To Sam and Will. Always be confident.

SECRETS OF CONFIDENT PEOPLE

The 50 Techniques You Need to Shine

Richard Nugent

First published in Great Britain in 2014 by Hodder & Stoughton. An Hachette UK company.

First published in US in 2014 by The McGraw-Hill Companies, Inc.

This edition published 2014

British Library Cataloguing in Publication Data: a catalogue record for this title is available from the British Library.

Library of Congress Catalog Card Number: on file.

Paperback ISBN: 9781473600065

ebook ISBN: 9781473600089

10 9 8 7 6 5 4 3 2 1

Typeset by Cenveo® Publisher Services.

Printed and bound in Great Britain by CPI Group (UK) Ltd., Croydon, CRO 4YY.

Hodder & Stoughton policy is to use papers that are natural, renewable and recyclable products and made from wood grown in sustainable forests. The logging and manufacturing processes are expected to conform to the environmental regulations of the country of origin.

Hodder & Stoughton Ltd

338 Euston Road

London NW1 3BH

www.hodder.co.uk

Also available in ebook

CONTENTS

This SECRETS book contains a number of special textual features, which have been developed to help you navigate the chapters quickly and easily. Throughout the book, you will find these indicated by the following icons.

 Each chapter contains quotes from inspiring figures. These will be useful for helping you understand different viewpoints and why each secret is useful in a practical context.

 Also included in each chapter are a number of strategies that outline techniques for putting this secret into practice.

 The putting it all together box at the end of each chapter provides a summary of each chapter, and a quick way into the core concepts of each secret.

12
13
(14)
15

You'll also see a chapter ribbon down the right hand side of each right-hand page, to help you mark your progress through the book and to make it easy to refer back to a particular chapter you found useful or inspiring.

INTRODUCTION

The importance of a book like this was captured perfectly for me by one of the contributors to it, a highly rated senior executive in one of the country's largest organizations. As a footnote to his fantastic and insightful chapter that will help others to be more confident, he added, 'It's ironic that I am doing this because I don't really feel confident'.

For most people confidence is context specific. We feel confident in some environments, with some people and in some situations but experience a complete lack of it in others. This book has been written to reverse that experience. You have the capacity to experience confidence in any situation and at any time. This book provides 50 techniques to help trigger and develop your natural confidence.

Confidence not arrogance

I have included a chapter which deals specifically with how to develop true deep confidence rather than a superficial surface version of it. It is crucial to differentiate between confidence and arrogance. It is impossible to be too confident. As you will see in the pages ahead, true confidence is humble; it helps you to share the limelight with others and is at times vulnerable. I often consider the most confident people to be those who feel comfortable with not feeling confident in a particular situation. Once you cross the line into self-importance, self-indulgence and ego-driven thinking and behaviour you have stepped out of confidence. The proper application of the techniques in this book is unlikely to lead to arrogance, but if you happen to stray across that line then take a swift step back as arrogance damages confidence.

My journey

One of the barriers to some people accessing their confidence is that they think other people can do it because of circumstance, education or even genetics. Because of this I want to be clear that I haven't always been an expert on confidence. I faced the same challenges with weight, bad skin and failed fledgling romances as most adolescents. I got my first job as a business trainer in my early twenties and while my career was fairly successful, moments of confidence were at a premium. Even my early days as a consultant were a rollercoaster of confidence-related emotions. Only in my early thirties when I discovered the fundamental secret of confidence did these peaks and troughs even out. I hope this book provides you with the same certainty that your confidence is in your hands.

How to get the most from this book

For most people this will be more of a selection box than a formal meal. Each chapter has been created so that anyone can learn from it, but undoubtedly some chapters will be more important or compelling to you. Read these first.

Remember that the whole concept of this book, and indeed the other books in this series, is to provide techniques that you can experiment with. Reading without action may lead to an unconscious increase in the amount of time you feel truly confident. By choosing a technique or two at a time and using them, I am confident that your confidence will grow significantly no matter what your starting point is!

While you will prioritize the order in which you read the chapters, I would encourage you to read the whole book. Each chapter contains valuable insights – even if you don't think the chapter title applies to you right now. For example, the chapter 'The confident comedian' contains some fantastic advice on how to trigger day-to-day confidence for those with no desire to tread the comedy boards.

Repetition is good

Some concepts and techniques will be repeated in various places through the book. This is completely intended. Repetition is the mother of all skill. Mastery relies at least in part on replicating good habits. If you notice a specific point is recurrent, perhaps it one that you need to learn most.

ACKNOWLEDGEMENTS

I am hugely grateful to many people for their input and support to bring this book into reality.

The wonderful contributers including Joanne Nugent, Martyn Beauchamp, Alexis Bowman, Jenny Bersin, Ray Biggs, Kevin Cherry, Steve Marriott, Graeme Carrick, James O'Connor, Nick Grantham, Haider Imam, and Brian Lumsdon and Ben Morton, my colleagues at TwentyOne Leadership.

Those who have influenced my work over recent years including Kimberley Hare, Michael Neill, Michael Heppell, Alastair Olby and Sue Bridgewater.

My wonderful support team including my Executive Assistant Jo Smith and branding expert and office buddy Ross Aitken.

The team at Hodder and in particular the superb support from Jamie Joseph.

There are many more than space permits here.

Finally thank you for reading this book, applying the techniques and making the world a more confidence place.

Note: details of books cited, TED talks and other weblinks can be found at the end of the book under Further reading.

The fundamental secret of confidence

❝ *Confidence is contagious. So is lack of confidence.* Vince Lombardi

❝ *With confidence you have won before you started.* Marcus Garvey

❝ *Confidence is that feeling by which the mind embarks in great and honourable courses with a sure hope and trust in itself.*
Marcus Tullius Cicero

❝ *The only power that exists is inside ourselves.* Anne Rice

❝ *Self-confidence is the first requisite to great undertakings.*
Samuel Johnson

If you have bought this book, the chances are that you want more confidence in certain areas of your life. In my work over the last decade I have encountered tens of thousands of people, and confidence is one of the most common development areas. I have been fortunate enough to work with professional footballers and athletes, CEOs and executives from some of the biggest and best-known brands in the world, and many, despite their apparent success, still feel they lack confidence.

By applying the tools, techniques and principles you will read on the following pages, you will have all the confidence you could ever need in any situation. You will be able to share these strategies with colleagues and clients, friends and family and, best of all, be able to trigger instant confidence whenever you need it.

You can choose to use the book in two ways: you can read it from cover to cover, applying the frameworks that are most appropriate for you; or you can use the index to guide you and use it as a toolkit to develop the areas that you feel are most important.

Whichever approach you take, the most important thing is to experiment and practise the concepts that you read. Any change comes from habit and learning it occurs through action.

Each of the secrets in this book are valuable in their own right, but all are built on the foundation of a fundamental understanding of what confidence is. Most people are brought up believing that confidence is something that they have or don't have. This is not the case; we all have it and can trigger it in an instant.

Confidence is not something you have or don't have; it's something that you do or don't do.

REALIZE THAT IT'S NOT OUTSIDE, IT'S INSIDE

Somewhere back in time someone created some particularly unhelpful language about confidence. We talk about confidence as if it is something that sits outside of us and that we get. We don't say, 'If only I could get more happy', yet we use that language about confidence. This leads to the misperception that we can only have confidence when a specific set of circumstances occur or when we have achieved certain things. We think that we will be confident when we are an expert in something or when we have lost a certain amount of weight, when we have achieved a promotion or gained a qualification. None of this is true.

Confidence is an emotional state. It is something that we feel sometimes and don't feel at other times. The various chapters outline the numerous ways in which we can feel this state more often, but it is really important to understand these strategies are triggers for the physical, mental and emotional state that we recognize as confidence.

UNDERSTANDING STATES

How long do you think states last? You might think that feelings take time to change. In fact, most emotional states last somewhere between 20 seconds and two minutes. All states are a result of an electrochemical reaction in the brain. These reactions are triggered by a combination of what you are thinking about, what you are doing with your body and your perception of the world around you.

States can be triggered in an instant and changed again in another and the great news is that you are completely in charge of your state at any time. We do, however, have certain states that we hang around in more of the time. I am sure that you can picture someone now who has a default state of miserable. They only seem to notice the negative in their world, they will always focus on what is bad or what could go wrong. They will answer a simple 'How are you?' with a low-energy, 'Oh surviving ... just'. These masters of misery will even have a specific posture and way of walking that radiates gloom. It is a state that they can access easily and do so regularly.

Now think of someone who seems to be in a consistently confident state. Think about how they see the world, what do they notice most in situations and who do they surround themselves with? What kind of language do you hear them using most? Now picture them walking across a room or sitting in a meeting. I bet that their physiology is significantly different from our melancholy friend from the first example.

When you remember that confidence is a feeling we get as a result of what we think, do and say, it is easy to see how people who understand this can be confident in any situation and find it easier and easier to get into that state.

FINDING YOUR STATE OF CONFIDENCE

Everyone is confident in some area of his or her life. If you have a job, can drive, have a family, play sport, are part of a club, or if you have ever done anything well – you know how to 'do' confidence. The secret is to know what your confidence looks, sounds and feels like and then replicate it in areas where you don't do confidence as easily.

Try this experiment. Think back to a time when you felt at your most confident best. It can be in any situation. Recall it as if you were there again now. See what you saw at that time, notice what is happening around you. It is important to be in the memory rather than watching it from outside. Keep focusing on the memory and notice the kinds of things you were thinking; if you were speaking remember the words that you were using and how you were saying them. Now, as you remember this time from the past when you were at your most confident best, focus on how you were standing or moving and, most importantly, how you were feeling. Notice where the confident feelings were in your body and how those feelings moved.

Now notice that, even though you were just accessing a memory, you are feeling some of that feeling right now. This is a taste of your confidence.

The brain is an amazing piece of kit that we are gaining a greater understanding of than ever before but the one thing that it doesn't do well is differentiate between what is real and what is strongly imagined. We will explore much more of the implications and uses of this inability in other chapters; however, the most important consequence of this in relation to confidence is that when we imagine ourselves as confident the brain releases the same chemicals around the body as when we really do feel confident. As you will see in future chapters the debate about 'we fake confidence' has no practical value.

Putting it all together

Confidence is a feeling that we get as a result of what we think, what we do with our body and how we perceive the world around us. These combine to create a neurological and biological response in the body. When the right mix of chemicals has the right receptors in the body we feel confident. This means that confidence can be triggered by us at any time regardless of situation, experience or external factors.

States are completely transient, changing moment by moment. We can influence these changes through our thinking, our physiology and our language. We can create structures and habits that ensure that confidence is a state that we default to. The more time you spend in any state the easier it is to re-access this state. It is important to remember that lack of confidence, fear and doubt are states that can become habit too.

You already are confident in many areas of your life even if you don't realize it. Noticing what confidence looks, sounds and feels like for you and then replicating this in other situations is a great way to build your confidence habit. This is especially useful because the brain processes reality, imagination and memory in the same way. If you imagine or remember confidence it will trigger it in the present.

These core principles and practices underpin the practical secrets that are shared in the rest of the book. Without this understanding of what confidence is and how it is created it would be much more difficult to apply the techniques presented here. Now that you have this understanding triggering your confidence will be easier than ever before.

2 The myth of fear

If confidence is a state then what is fear? When people define it they usually refer back to times in the past when they experienced fear, but they don't define what it actually is. Fear is a feeling, or we would label it a state. As with any other emotional state it is triggered by a combination of what you do with your body, the words and phrases that you use and, importantly, the thoughts that you concentrate most on.

We believe that we get afraid because of other people or because of certain situations but this is not the case. Our fear is triggered because of what we think about certain situations or people.

Take phobias as an example. My younger brother has a phobia of clowns. Even seeing a picture of a clown will trigger an almost overwhelming sense of fear and the physiological reactions that come with it including increased heart rate, body temperature and instant perspiring. If you asked him why he is so afraid of clowns he would tell you it was because they are weird looking and scary and he just is. There was an instant when James was a very small child that he saw a clown at a party and was frightened by it. He can't actually remember that event, so it isn't the memory of the clown that triggers fear. He has a connection in his brain that he is scared of clowns. His fear is a result of a thought he has, not an external event.

It is worth remembering that these kinds of thoughts seem real. Because of this the feelings of fear that we experience feel very real. Highly confident people have a way of experiencing this fear and moving on from it quickly and by using the techniques in the rest of this chapter you can too.

LEARN HOW YOU TRIGGER YOUR FEAR

The first step in escaping fear is to be clear about how you create it. In order to create the state of fear you must be imagining whatever you are thinking about going badly. For example, if you are feeling fear about a presentation you are going to do, you must be imagining this presentation going badly. It is this negative future thinking that triggers the sense of fear. Even in what appears to be a live situation it is your thinking about what is going to happen that triggers fear. If someone walks towards you in a way that you consider to be threatening, it is not their walk that creates alarm, it is what you are imagining is going to happen next that triggers those feelings. Next time you feel a sense of fear, spend a moment noticing what specifically you are thinking about. I guarantee you are imagining a situation going badly. The more vividly you are running the mental DVD through your head, the stronger your fear reaction will be. Similarly the more times you repeat these pictures and sounds in your mind, the more real they will become and so will your sense of fear.

TAKE THE ANTIDOTE

It is worth understanding at this stage that it is impossible to feel fear in the moment. Let's take the example of someone walking towards you in a threatening way. I hope this never happens to you, but if it did your fear is likely to be the result of you thinking that you are going to be attacked. However, if the worst happened you would not be feeling fear – or at least not of being attacked. You may be feeling fear about what is going to happen next – again this is future thinking.

In less extreme circumstances, such as work and social situations, the understanding that fear can't be felt in the moment is vital in providing an antidote. For example, when mentally rehearsing your presentation, if you notice the state of fear building, stop and consciously rewind the movie that has been running in your head. Now play it through your head in full sounds and colour again but with every element of the situation going brilliantly. You will notice the sense of fear fall away.

It is impossible to feel a real sense of fear while imagining any future situation going well or positively. Positive future mental rehearsal of any situation provides the antidote to fear in any situation.

USE FEAR WHEN IT IS USEFUL

Fear is a survival instinct. It is not useful to reverse every sense of fear we experience. A friend worked closely with a top security consultant in Hollywood. This personal safety expert suggested that when the rich and famous suffered personal harm it was almost always because they had ignored some warning signs that they were at risk or putting themselves in a dangerous situation.

Highly confident people don't ignore fear, but they do have a natural way of understanding when fear is rational, and when it is irrational and getting in the way of what they want to achieve.

Imagine for a moment that your state of fear is a living thing in itself. Its purpose is to get you to pay attention and take action. The action you take should be very different depending on when and where the fear shows up. Your fear appearing just as you start to walk down a dark and secluded shortcut home on your own is likely to be a signpost for a reroute. However when a sense of panic overwhelms you about a presentation you are due to make in six weeks' time then I would suggest that the attention you must pay is to prepare more fully, especially emotionally, for the event.

Putting it all together

In the same way that confidence is a state we trigger with our thoughts and physiology, our sense of fear is something that we can manage and change quickly and easily (with practice). Most of us are brought up with an understanding of fear as being something that is outside of us but instead it is our processing of a situation and, more accurately, our projection of future situations that create our own sense of fear.

The three secrets of fear that you have discovered during this chapter are:

1. You will only feel fear if you imagine something going badly or wrong.
2. It is impossible to feel fear 'in the moment'. If something bad happens the primary emotion tends not to be fear, at least not about what is actually happening.
3. You can't feel fear while imagining a situation or event going well.

The lesson from highly confident people is to reduce the occurrences of what emotional intelligence guru Daniel Goleman calls the 'amygdala hijack'. Goleman uses the term to describe emotional responses from people which are immediate, overwhelming and out of proportion with the actual stimulus. The threat response (fear) that we experience is much greater than the threat itself.

Fear in itself isn't bad. In fact it is a protection mechanism that helps us stay alive, but irrational and uncontrolled fear is unhelpful and a significant barrier to real and continued confidence. Consider the situations in which you allow your fear to become an unhelpful barrier and use the antidote in this chapter to turn your experiences around.

I would also highly recommend to parents that you help your children understand this different version of fear at as early a stage as possible. So many young people have their potential inhibited by fears that are never likely to exist anywhere but in their minds and those of their teachers and parents.

9

3 Understand the power of your thoughts

❝ *The world as we have created it is a process of our thinking. It cannot be changed without changing our thinking.* Albert Einstein

❝ *We are addicted to our thoughts. We cannot change anything if we cannot change our thinking.* Santosh Kalwar

❝ *The spirit of the individual is determined by his dominating thought habits.* Bruce Lee

❝ *The beginning of wisdom is the definition of terms.* Socrates

❝ *Did you ever stop to think, and forget to start again?*
Winnie the Pooh

How much of what you understand as reality is a direct experience of what is happening in the outside world, and how much of what you experience as real is created in your head? I have asked this question at seminars and conferences up and down the country, and no one has ever answered that our experience of the world is one hundred per cent real and accurate.

Research by Shaun Achor from Harvard University suggests that around 90 per cent of what we experience is not the outside world but instead it is as a result of the lens that we see the world through.

Perhaps the fastest growing area of psychology in the world today is based on three fundamental principles of thought, mind and consciousness. These three principles (as originally defined by philosopher and author Sydney Banks) combine to create our experience. Those living by Banks's ethos are likely to suggest that 100 per cent of our experience is as a result of our thinking about world rather than the world itself.

Whichever of these schools of thought is closest to your understanding of how the world works, it is clear that what we think has a direct impact on our confidence. The thoughts we spend most time on will define our levels of confidence.

In simple terms, if you spend more time thinking about your shortcomings, what may go wrong and how people may perceive you negatively, then this will result in low confidence. If you spend more time thinking that people are perceiving you positively, what your strengths are and the potential positive results of what you do, then the higher your confidence will be. My experience in the world of sport and business tells me that people forget these certainties of confidence.

The good news is that understanding the impact of your thinking on your confidence means that you don't always have to change your thinking to be positive. Noticing that you are wrapped up in thoughts that are moving you out of a confidence state is often enough for these thoughts to have less energy and internal influence.

NOTICE YOUR THINKING ABOUT CONFIDENCE

The first step to influencing your thinking about confidence is to notice your thinking and become more aware of the thoughts that you have which move your confidence levels up or down. The following mini-project of noticing your thinking is one that I give to every new coaching client.

The next time that you notice a specific change in the amount of confidence you are feeling, take a moment to pause and become aware of what you have been thinking about. At this stage you don't have to do anything with these thoughts – this isn't a positive thinking exercise. The aim is just to notice what you are thinking.

Here is a simple example. You are getting ready for a big social occasion. You will spend the night with people who you really want to impress. You spend considerable time getting ready and before you're due to head out you check the mirror for a final time. You aren't happy. You spend the next five minutes studying every imperfection, whether it's extra weight, signs of ageing or lack of that all important symmetry that beautiful people have. You decide that your outfit isn't complimentary so make a rushed change. Another five-minute mirror check confirms it isn't the mirror, it is you. You quickly change again, take one last opportunity to notice everything that is wrong with you and then you rush out of the door with your confidence left on the floor with your rejected clothes.

Now imagine another day. You look in the mirror, notice that you look OK and leave. On the days when we think we look good we spend a really brief period thinking about how we look and on the bad days we spend lots of time.

It is not the image in front of us that decides our confidence in these situations but the thoughts we have about those images. The same applies to any of our thinking about confidence and in order to understand this you must first get used to noticing your thinking.

CHANGE YOUR FOCUS

Imagine you are in the cinema watching a scary movie. It is the moment that the film reaches its scariest moment; the fear gets a little too much for you. What do you do? Do you keep watching ever more intently? Do you stare at the very thing that is making you feel bad and analyse why you are feeling like that? Or do you simply turn away from the screen and concentrate on something else? We know a simple change in focus in this situation is all we need to do to shift our thinking and change how we feel in that moment.

Now consider the same approach to confidence. If you notice your thinking is creating a lack of confidence, the simplest strategy is to focus on something else. If you feel your thinking, then changing your thinking will naturally change how you feel – and in an instant.

Occasionally when I share this with people who have been used to thinking about confidence in the old way – as a belief that it is built and reinforced over years – they reject the idea that simply changing focus can create more confidence. If it sounds too easy to you, I would guess that this is because your current strategy is to focus on and examine in detail the thoughts that negatively affect your confidence. The more you are used to exploring these thoughts and immersing yourself in them, the more challenging you will find it to change your focus. If this seems familiar, then use other techniques in this book to increase your confidence but make changing your focus one that you revisit and practise.

THINK ABOUT THINKING ABOUT CONFIDENCE

When you think of being confident, how do you feel? Happy, hopeful, sad, frustrated? What about when you think about a lack of confidence? How do you experience that? One of the key traits of truly confident people that I have noticed over the years is how they feel when they don't have confidence. It is a myth to think that people who are highly confident are in a constantly confident state; it is more true to say that it matters much less when they don't feel confident. They don't attach any strong meaning to their momentary confidence dip. They don't connect the absence of confidence to their performance in whatever they are trying to do and, most importantly, they don't consider it as permanent.

When you really understand the impact of thinking on your confidence, then you are able to feel a lack of confidence and experience it as nothing more than that. Confidence is a state, as is lack of confidence. Both are useful in some situations and not in others. The ability to notice when you aren't confident, to notice your thinking about it and be completely OK with that lack of confidence, is in itself the ultimate experience of confidence.

Putting it all together

We are all living in the experience of our thinking.

The thoughts that we focus on most create our perception of what is real. This understanding is crucial in becoming more confident.

The more we revisit thoughts of confidence, the more we will experience ourselves in that way. The opposite is also true. Many people have developed a strong habit of focusing on thoughts that reinforce their self-perception as unconfident.

The regular practice of noticing your thinking will help you to understand how you create your sense of confidence or your lack of it. The more you do it, the more you will notice how much of this comes from your thinking about a situation or person rather than the situation or person itself.

Noticing your thinking will take the energy out of the thought that is creating your unhelpful feeling. However, changing your focus – literally thinking about something else – will naturally interrupt the thought pattern that is creating a negative feeling.

Being comfortable with a temporary absence of confidence is a sign of confidence.

The experience of understanding that a lack of confidence is nothing more than the absence of a specific state and not something that you should link to your identity or performance is the ultimate step in understanding the power of thought and its impact on confidence.

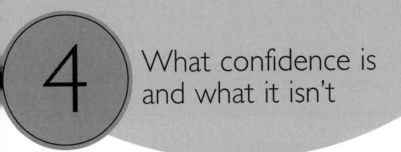

4 What confidence is and what it isn't

Arrogance is blind to the stumbling block. Toba Beta, *Master of Stupidity*

Arrogance makes you stronger from outside, but weaker inside.
Ujas Soni

Rookies tend to show off. Toba Beta, *Master of Stupidity*

Knowing others is wisdom, knowing yourself is Enlightenment.
Lao Tzu

Confidence is the mark of a hopeful disposition. Aristotle

So far in this book we have established that confidence is a
neurological and physiological state that can be triggered by a
combination of what we do with our body and what thoughts
we pay most attention to. You will notice that so far we have
given little attention to our behaviours beyond these foundations.
While we will examine the habits of interaction later in the
book, it is important to remain clear that confidence is a largely
inside-out experience.

Over the past ten years my clients have included CEOs and
executives from multimillion pound and dollar organizations. I have
worked with professional sportsmen and women at the peak of
their careers who perform in front of tens of thousands of people
week in and week out. You would think that these people were
all masters of their self-confidence; however, too many of these
people were relying on an outside-in version of confidence that is
often then perceived by others as arrogance. You have probably
felt it about someone in the past. That nagging sense that this is all

a front, like all you are seeing of that person is a brightly coloured shell hiding the real person inside. There is a fine but significant line between self-generated confidence and this fragile superiority. Worst of all, the outside-in nature of this self-protection blocks the building of true and lasting confidence habits.

NOTICE WHEN YOU'RE AT YOUR MOST CONFIDENT

How do you know you have done something well? Is it as a result of feedback, the obvious achievement of results or do you just know? Some of us are naturally wired in such a way that we rely mainly on external sources to let us know whether we have done a good job or not. For these people the main source of understanding about their performance in any area of their life lies in the hands of others. This can be hugely challenging when it comes to building your confidence from the inside. If you are the kind of person that gets huge energy from feedback others give you, it is especially important that you build your own self-confidence routines.

A brilliant way to do this is to make a habit of noticing daily successes or moments when you have felt at your most confident. It may be useful for you to make a daily practice of writing the successes, or 'confidence moments', from the previous day as a way of setting yourself up positively for the day ahead. This will trigger states of confidence in the moment and also begin to rewire your brain to notice more of those moments as they happen.

This process can also be useful for those of us who are wired to use our own internal criteria to define whether something has been a success or not. People with this preference – known as internally referenced – know themselves better than anyone else whether they have done a good job or not. Internally referenced people don't get the same energy from feedback or external criteria as those who are externally referenced. My experience is that internally referenced people can find it easier to build a bank of positive experience; however, if they go through a prolonged period where they don't feel things are going well they can also give undue weight to these experiences.

If you have a tendency to feel that enough is never good enough or you suffer from the curse of perfectionism then it is even more important that you notice your thinking about how you have performed at a certain task in a specific situation (see Chapter 2).

BE A WEEBLE

Those of you of a certain age will remember the Weeble. The Weeble was an egg-shaped child's toy with a weight on the bottom. The marketing tagline was 'Weebles wobble but they don't fall down'. This is a great metaphor for the building of real confidence as opposed to arrogance.

People who operate from this frail, surface false confidence build it up like scaffolding around them. It holds them up in certain situations or in certain company. It often looks bold and sounds loud. It is self-important and is fuelled by talk of achievements or connections with these who are achieving.

However when the person is taken out of the comfort zone that this scaffolding is built for, it falls away leaving a vulnerable and often overwhelmed person.

By applying the knowledge and tools from this book you can be sure you are becoming a Weeble. Your internal resources provide a solid but flexible base of confidence that is with you no matter what the circumstances and even when you don't feel confident in the moment, you know that you can be with the next thought or action.

With this real base of inside-out confidence you can let go of your ego. You don't have to prove how confident you are by talking up your achievements, how much money you have or who you know. True confidence enables you to show up as your best self more often and more comfortably.

MAKE GREAT COFFEE

There is one secret of confidence that almost every book and resource I have read seems to ignore. Being brilliant at something is a great builder of confidence. I have met lots of people who are talented and try to ignore it but in general the burden of evidence becomes so great that they finally give in and allow their confidence to grow. My friend and mentor Michael Neill used to share his principles for building a great coaching business as part of his coaching seminars. Among the principles for gaining clients and developing your profile was always the line 'make great coffee'. In other words, to build a great coaching business you must give people great coaching.

We can apply the same principle to any area of life. If you lack confidence when presenting (more on this later in the book) then apply the learning from this book to grow your confidence in this area, but also develop your presentation style and skills. The better you become the more your confidence will grow. This isn't rocket science, but the role of personal and professional development is one of the pillars of confidence that is often overlooked.

Putting it all together

We all appreciate some kind of external recognition of our skills and the work that we do. When we get this appreciation it helps trigger a more powerful confidence state. It is important to hold on to the fact that confidence still comes as a result of what we do and think. The habit of focusing on success experiences or moments of confidence is hugely valuable in the process of cementing confidence as a default state.

Highly confident people aren't permanently at a 10/10 level of confidence. During my time with the business consultancy Kaizen Training, one of the attributes we would look for in a new recruit was 'the ability to light up a room but not to have to'. Truly confident people will be comfortable in the moments when stuff happens and their confidence temporarily fades. They will also be comfortable when the spotlight is on others, knowing that their turn will come and not be driven by their ego to wrestle the spotlight back.

You can only ignore the fact that you are brilliant at something for so long. Eventually the results will cancel out your lack of confidence in that particular area of your life. Think for a moment about your particular areas of professional or personal expertise. It is likely that you know 90 per cent more than 90 per cent of the people on the planet on a number of subjects. The better and more consistent results you get the more your confidence will grow.

5 The official psychology of confidence

❝ *Wanting to be someone else is a waste of the person you are.*
Marilyn Monroe

❝ *Don't belittle yourself. Be BIG yourself.* Corita Kent

❝ *In order to succeed, people need a sense of self-efficacy, to struggle together with resilience to meet the inevitable obstacles and inequities of life.* Albert Bandura

❝ *There are no constraints on the human mind, no walls around the human spirit, no barriers to our progress except those we ourselves erect.* Ronald Reagan

❝ *Make the most of yourself, for that is all there is of you.*
Ralph Waldo Emerson

We know confidence is an emotional state. We recognize that the feeling created from the biological process can be triggered instantly and anchored by habits that help this to become a default state. This understanding of confidence is quite a recent one and I think that there is value in exploring a more traditional psychological view of it.

Psychologists rarely measure confidence as a single entity. Instead they measure three factors:

- **Self-esteem** – A measure of the degree to which an individual values themselves.
- **Narcissism** – A destructive form of high self-esteem.
- **Self-efficacy** – The ability to achieve personal goals.

In various research journals there is dispute between the impacts of these various areas on the success of individuals, so the traditional view on confidence becomes a difficult one to apply in practice. The more contemporary view is that a balance of the two positive traits and the avoidance of narcissism leads to happiness and contributes to success.

An over-reliance on self-esteem alone, without any focus on the achievement of goals, can lead to shorter term confidence that is undermined by a sense of under-achievement. Many self-help books in the late 90s and early 2000s overplayed the focus on just feeling good without a need for action.

Too great a focus on the achievement of goals will lead to an uncomfortable success. We explore in other chapters of this book how an over-emphasis in this area creates the potential for our achievements to overtake the levels of genuine confidence we have in ourselves.

When we value ourselves and the contribution we make to others around us (self-esteem), and we have belief that we can succeed (self-efficacy), then we create a great breeding ground for confidence.

It is an excellent reminder that confidence is a positive and desirable state to be in and to be around. It is neither self-loving nor negative to others. Narcissism and confidence are in some ways opposites.

MAINTAIN YOUR SELF-ESTEEM

Many studies have been carried out into self-esteem over the years. These studies suggest that our baseline level of self-esteem is significantly impacted upon by environmental factors such as social class, maturation, birth order and gender. This could leave us with a belief that self-esteem can't be affected significantly; however, many studies also show that our level of self-esteem is created by our reflections of performance across a range of areas. This gives us the ability to focus on the areas of our life that we perform best in, in order to build a general self-value. It also shows the importance of learning and development in increasing our self-worth.

Take the time now to list and reflect on the areas of your life that you perform well in. For some of you this will be an easy task. For others, you may find it difficult to identify them. If this is the case, then break down the task that you are good at into smaller and smaller elements. I can find no scientific evidence that suggests that more important performance areas carry more weight in their influence of our self-esteem. In other words if you make brilliant coffee and others appreciate it, your focus on this could still impact on your self-esteem just as much as a focus on something that technically has more social significance.

AVOID NARCISSISM

At the core of narcissism is a preoccupation with one's self. Narcissism is revealed by an unhealthy focus on personal preferences, aspirations, needs, success, and how one is perceived by others. In the extreme, narcissists tend to become physically and emotionally isolated.

I would expect few narcissists to be reading a book on confidence, so a strategy for battling self-obsession seems a little unnecessary. However, this is an opportunity to highlight again that real confidence is a positive social state. Those who master genuine confidence do not need to feed their ego. They know they are fundamentally 'OK' and therefore are able to be vulnerable. Confident people are able to focus on others because of their comfort with themselves.

If at any point your future success leads you to fall into any narcissistic traits here are three simple ways to come back from the brink.

Judge all people as the same. We are all intelligent and highly functioning forms of flesh and bone powered by electricity and mysterious life force. Beyond that money, status, IQ or other means that we use to judge others are created in our own heads.

Laugh at yourself. We all do silly things. Every person has made a crazy decision or made a temporary fool of themselves. Take time to reflect on how you have made others smile through these things.

Give service in any way that you can. There are few ways to become more humble than to give what you can to others. The narcissistic way is to be so focused on self that they don't see the needs of others. My wife and I recently gave some old toys to a local women's refuge. While we were happy to help it was an incredibly humbling experience to remember how lucky we are and to see more of the challenges of others.

BUILD BELIEF IN YOUR ABILITY TO GET THE JOB DONE

Self-efficacy is one of the best defined areas in traditional psychology's view of confidence. The work of Albert Bandura gives us a great platform to understand what those high in self-efficacy do, what those with a lack of it are prone to and, most importantly, how to build it.

Bandura defines self-efficacy as 'the belief in one's capabilities to organize and execute the courses of action required to manage prospective situations'. Put simply the degree of certainty that we have the ability to do, what we need to, to achieve what we want to.

People with a strong sense of self-efficacy:

- view challenging problems as tasks to be mastered
- develop deeper interest in the activities in which they participate
- form a stronger sense of commitment to their interests and activities
- recover quickly from setbacks and disappointments.

Most people have things they want to accomplish or achieve. Most people also understand that putting these plans into action is not quite as easy. Bandura and others have found that people who have the traits of strong self-efficacy will approach goals, tasks, and challenges very differently to those who demonstrate traits of low self-efficacy.

People with a low sense of self-efficacy:

- avoid challenging tasks
- believe that difficult tasks and situations are beyond their capabilities

- focus on personal failings and negative outcomes
- quickly lose confidence in personal abilities.

Bandura also outlines how those with high self-efficacy build that characteristic. Here are four sub-strategies to help you build your belief in your ability to complete a specific task.

1. Mastery experiences. Complete the task successfully to the point that it is mastered.
2. Social modelling. Witnessing other people successfully completing the task is another important source of self-efficacy. This especially applies when observing people in a similar position who have to strive to complete the task.
3. Social persuasion. Bandura found that people could be persuaded to believe that they have the skills and capabilities to succeed. Consider who you could enlist to persuade you that you can do a particular task.
4. Psychological responses. Paying attention to how you feel before completing a task and using some of the tools contained in this book will in themselves contribute to the belief that you can achieve it. As you will have read in other chapters in this book, emotional states are often self-fulfilling.

Putting it all together

This book is full of techniques to build and solidify your confidence. These strategies have been created by modelling those who are already confident and codifying the results. Traditionalists who are rightly protective of psychology can challenge this approach and its reputation.

This chapter confirms that the techniques included in this book complement the traditional view of confidence rather than conflict with it. Indeed this alternative way of categorizing the approaches you can employ will help ensure that your confidence continues to grow. This inclusion of narcissism as a characteristic to avoid provides a boundary and sense check.

Much of the early formal research into the elements of confidence suggested that many of the factors involved were predicated on environmental factors such as upbringing. It is clear from more recent research and social experiments that confidence comes from within and can indeed be built.

The most important person in deciding how well or easy it is to develop your confidence is you. You have to find the approaches that work for you. No book or academic can give you the exact formula, but with a small amount of effort and a fair amount of experimentation you will crack your confidence code.

6 Who are you?

> As you become more clear about who you really are, you'll be better able to decide what is best for you – the first time around. **Oprah Winfrey**

> Your vision will become clear only when you can look into your own heart. Who looks outside, dreams; who looks inside, awakes. **Carl Jung**

> To keep the body in good health is a duty ... otherwise we shall not be able to keep our mind strong and clear. **Buddha**

> Truth is by nature self-evident. As soon as you remove the cobwebs of ignorance that surround it, it shines clear.
> **Mahatma Gandhi**

> We know what we are, but not what we may be. **William Shakespeare**

To help get to grips with the concept of identity I want to start this chapter with a question. The only answer that you aren't allowed to give to this question is your own name. Here is the question.

Who are you?

If you have tried to answer that question, then you will know that it is deceptively difficult. It gets straight to the heart of your character, personality and individuality.

Your self-identity is a key factor in defining the areas of your life where confidence is likely to be naturally high and the situations in which you will have to work at it. I recently worked with a professional footballer. Despite the fact that he was married and had children, when asked to answer the identity question he clearly said that he was 'just a footballer'. It is no surprise then that he was hugely confident on the training pitch, in the dressing room and during games; however, the thought of attending a local charity event and giving a short speech about the work he did sent his confidence through the floor.

Your self-identity will define what you think you are capable of doing, what you believe about yourself and the world, and what is most important to you in situations; it even influences what you do. All of this from a concept that has grown and been defined unconsciously over the course of your life.

BE AWARE OF YOUR IDENTITIES

It is time for another identity exercise. Write down a list of the life roles that you regularly adopt.

Here are some examples of roles that I adopt.

Dad	Brother	Manager
Family bank manager	Cleaner	Taxi driver
Friend	Footballer	Writer
Coach	Gardener	Furniture construction expert

If you review your identities you will understand that what is important in some won't be in others. Your abilities in some roles will be really high, but really low in others. Some of these identities will be chosen and others will be forced upon you.

You will also appreciate that in some life roles your confidence will flow naturally and in others you will have to use the tools in this book to trigger it. This goes beyond how you perceive your abilities to do the tasks related to the role, and is defined by how you see yourself in relation to the role.

While this concept of identity impacting on confidence is not gender specific, my experience is that there are more opportunities for it to impact females than males.

A familiar example of this came from a client I worked with who had recently become a mother. Her self-identity was one of a Human Resources Director from well before her job title reflected this. She excelled in her studies and career and sure enough became the youngest HR Director in her company's history. Then, following a surprise pregnancy, she became a mother and after six months returned to work to find everything had changed. When I first met her she shared how decisions that once were easy to make required huge consideration. She felt that her values were very different and this impacted on her ability do be effective in her role. Consider for a moment the identity of a mum and the values, beliefs and capabilities that must come to the fore. Compare them to the values, beliefs and capabilities that are most important as an HR Director. They are clearly different and at times will conflict. Everyone who is a parent faces these conflicts.

ADOPT AN IDENTITY TO BOOST CONFIDENCE

This creation and change of identities is happening at a deeply unconscious level pretty much all the time. By making it more conscious then we can use our different life roles to increase our confidence in many different situations. You are effectively borrowing your confidence from one area of your life and applying it in another.

Revisit the list of life roles you created earlier. Which of these would you consider that you are most confident in? When you are in this role and feeling highly confident, what is that like? Where in your body do you feel that confidence? How does that confidence manifest in your thinking and how you behave?

Now think of another of your life roles. Imagine applying that confidence in that role. What impact would that have? How would you be acting if you adopted the confidence from the previous identity to that role?

Making this thought process part of your preparation for specific situations will be a powerful way to ensure that your confidence is consistent and feels congruent as you are simply expanding your natural confidence.

CREATE ASPIRATIONAL IDENTITIES

My friend, coach and mentor Michael Neill helped me learn a valuable lesson about self-identity a number of years ago. He shared a story of being challenged about a strapline on his website. It read 'one of the world's best success coaches', and a close friend suggested the he remove 'one of' from all his literature. For a brief time Michael protested, arguing that there was no sure-fire way of measuring his abilities and results against others. When he was finally convinced to make the change he immediately found that he thought and operated differently as the need to inhabit his new identity of 'the world's best success coach' took hold.

This is just one of many examples of people I have met living into a new and aspirational identity. Don't wait until you are completely comfortable with a self-identity before thinking about how you would operate if that were true.

As I write this book, if I adopt the identity of a coach who coaches on confidence I notice that my beliefs are that I can write some useful tips and ideas, that it is important that I do my best to make them simple to follow and that I need to work hard to write a great book. Frankly it doesn't feel inspiring.

Now, what if I adopt the identity of 'the world's foremost expert on helping anyone master confidence in every area of their life'? I have already noticed a change in how I feel inside. I believe that I have enough knowledge, tools, techniques and useful information for two books and that every person who reads it will improve their life by applying what they read. It is my duty to get this knowledge out there so I've suddenly got huge energy to get the best of what I know down in writing. Just by exploring a different identity I have a totally different experience of my confidence about writing even though that identity may not be completely true. Of course, if I write the world's most amazing book then that identity could become a self-fulfilling prophecy!

How can you apply this in your life? Explore it in your identities around work, parenting or relationships.

Putting it all together

Your self-identity influences which values, beliefs and capabilities are prevalent at any particular time. We all have different identities and we will experience more or less confidence in these identities at different times in our lives. By becoming really aware of which of these versions of our personality we operate in most often and in which we are more resourceful we can borrow confidence from one area of our lives and apply it in another.

This exploration of the different versions of ourselves can be extended by considering what identities it would be useful for us to live into. It is important not to be completely incongruent when exploring new identities but instead to think about how we can stretch and expand what is there already.

This is a great time to stop and ask the question 'who am I when I am at my best?'

7 You and your values

Too many people over value what they are not and under value what they are. Malcolm S. Forbes

Your beliefs become your thoughts, Your thoughts become your words,
Your words become your actions, Your actions become your habits,
Your habits become your values, Your values become your destiny.
Mahatma Gandhi

Sticking to your values, listening to your instincts, making your own choices is so important. Brittany Murphy

We cannot think of being acceptable to others until we have first proven acceptable to ourselves. Malcolm X

Start where you are.
Use what you have.
Do what you can. Arthur Ashe

Personal values are a representation of what is really important to us in life. While this book aims to share the secrets of highly confident people, in this chapter I can share with certainty a common trait of the unconfident. Living with behaviours that contravene your values will drain your sense of confidence.

This applies in relationships when the things that are most important to one partner aren't important to the other. In business, employees who are forced to operate under a set of values that they don't share will quickly become disengaged. Families who don't have a set of shared values — explicit or implicit — will quickly fall apart.

31

The first challenge for most people is that they don't have the opportunity to define what their values are. You will intuitively know what is most important to you, but it is unlikely that you will have defined your values clearly and even less likely that you have shared them with others.

Having a network of people around you who share the same sense of what is really important in work, relationships or life will naturally give you confidence. Their behaviours are more likely to be congruent with yours. The choices they make will align with yours and even if they have different character traits you have the foundation of a solid relationship.

When my wife and I analysed a number of our key character traits it confirmed that we are on opposite ends of the scale on many of them. She likes detail, I like the big picture. She likes certainty, I like variety. She does most of her thinking on the inside, I form ideas out loud. The list goes on and on. So what has held us together through over a decade of marriage? A shared view on what is most important really.

UNCOVER YOUR VALUES

We have established that your values are a representation of what is most important to you really. I have encountered lots of processes over the years to elicit personal values and my favourite is still the simplest. It is most powerfully done in an environment you are comfortable in and at a time that you won't be interrupted.

Take five or ten minutes to answer the following question: *what is most important to me really?* Typically people will list somewhere between four and eight things. They shouldn't be materialistic things. If your list includes your shiny new car then I would suggest that you aren't thinking deeply enough. Don't over-analyze as you are writing, go with whatever comes up first. I find that intuition plays a useful part in the process.

Once you have your list then take a further moment to review each one and get clear on what that actually means to you. Here are some examples from my values.

Honesty: Be straightforward in conversations. This doesn't mean being rude, but I love people with whom what you see is what you get. The opposite of this is lying and that is likely to create hurt or anger.

Variety: Trying new things and going to new places is important and gives me energy. Routines have their place but not routine for the sake of it.

Family: This is one of the most difficult for me to articulate because family is the single most important thing to me. My children, wife, parents and siblings form the cornerstones upon which everything else is built.

If you have followed this simple process you now have a clear articulation of your values. By being consciously aware of what is most important to you, you will notice others demonstrating their values through their actions and decisions.

THE POWER OF COMMONLY SHARED VALUES.

I have already shared one example of the power of shared values in relationships. I'm not suggesting the first-date protocol of comparing lists of what is important really, but it is worth paying attention to the things that a new partner seems to make a priority and compare this with your values. I think it is perfectly acceptable, in fact desirable, to have a values-led conversation in an established relationship. This can be especially useful during challenging times in a partnership. Temporary lapses in behaviour can be overcome, but differences in value sets are a much greater challenge.

In business, the impact of shared values is equally clear. Research carried out by James Kouzes and Barry Posner found that discussing personal values in organizations creates a significantly greater sense of engagement among employees than discussing the company's values. (*The Leadership Challenge*, Kouzes and Posner).

My work in organizations has led to the certain belief that company values should be a representation of the most commonly shared values of the people in that organization.

When this is the case the values will naturally come to life and be lived and breathed throughout the business. In coaching senior executives I always recommend that if their values don't at least overlap with their company's values they should leave the organization before this incongruence drains their energy and confidence, and negatively impacts on the business.

Your values strongly influence your behaviours and decisions. Surrounding yourself with people who share your values naturally validates your behaviours and decisions, and reinforces your sense of confidence.

TURN VALUES INTO BEHAVIOURS

Now that you are clear on the things that are most important to you really, use them to drive your behaviours. What should you be doing more of if these are your values? What must you do less of? One of the biggest drains on confidence is the sense that you have to do things or behave in ways that are in conflict with your values.

If you are a leader of a team or organization, use the shared values of that entity to define which behaviours are acceptable and which aren't. For example in my organization one of our values is 'balance'. This is a representation of the shared values the team have around the importance of work–life balance, health and family. When we make decisions about which projects to work on these values drive our behaviour and influences our decisions. If a project is long or particularly intense then it is a must that the team member takes specific recovery time during and after it. It is also OK for any team member to turn down a project to honour the value of balance.

Putting it all together

Values are the things that are most important to us really and form the basis of much of our unconscious decision making. Living a life at odds with your values will guarantee you unhappiness and lead to a lack of confidence. Spending too much time with people who don't share your values has the same impact. Over time your values may shift and this leaves you with choices to make about how and where you spend your time. Be brave in these choices as they can define how fulfilled your life is.

To the uninitiated, values can seem somewhat fluffy but as your understanding of values grows so will your appreciation of their importance. One of the most interesting challenges is to avoid judging those whose value set is different from yours. These people can seem odd and give you the sense of a distorted view of life. The reality is that they just hold different things to be important than you do. When you begin to see this more clearly and accept it then your confidence will make a significant leap.

Remain clear as to what your values are. Work on building friendships, relationships and careers that allow you to live these values more freely, and encourage others to do the same. Values-led relationships and organizations are always the most successful. Ensure yours are among these.

8 It's not all about you

> ❝ *Listening is a positive act: you have to put yourself out to do it.*
> **David Hockney**

> ❝ *I like to listen. I have learned a great deal from listening carefully. Most people never listen.* **Ernest Hemingway**

> ❝ *When you really listen to another person from their point of view, and reflect back to them that understanding, it's like giving them emotional oxygen.* **Stephen Covey**

> ❝ *If you make listening and observation your occupation you will gain much more than you can by talk.* **Robert Baden-Powell**

> ❝ *Most of the successful people I've known are the ones who do more listening than talking.* **Bernard Baruch**

It is a common misconception that confident people have to be the life and soul of every room at all times. When I started my career as a business consultant, one of the behaviours I was measured against was 'can light up a room but doesn't have to'. I think this articulates the approach of the genuinely confident. They know they can bring energy and be at the centre of a conversation, but don't feel that they have to be. The inability to share the limelight often has its roots in the fear that you won't be able to step out of another's shadow. On other occasions it can be a lack of social intelligence which leaves others sensing an overbearing nature. I experienced this at a recruitment event I led with a group of colleagues. One of the participants had a particularly strong CV and track record. On paper he seemed too good to be true. Unfortunately during the event he showed this to be the case. In every group exercise, and during breaks at lunch, he dominated the conversation and gave others little opportunity to contribute to the discussion. While this showed a surface confidence, it also demonstrated a lack of awareness especially as we were looking for as many good candidates as possible. In the final wrap up of the day he again monopolized the open session, asking three questions in quick succession, and on each occasion he addressed me as Robert despite us having several one-to-one conversations and him having full information on each assessor.

Confidence isn't dominating or overpowering. The confident person knows when to focus their attention on others and be a conduit for that person's confidence. While this chapter will largely concentrate on specific strategies to do this, the first step is to set a clear intention within yourself that you are going focus your attention on others. For many people this doesn't happen naturally and it takes patience and conscious effort especially in situations where others are vying for attention.

My experience is that the long-term impact is positive. Confident people don't have to light up the room, because they are secure in the knowledge they can at any time. It is those who lack confidence that court attention, as if it is the last time they will ever experience it.

SEE THEM

How often do you begin an interaction with the sole intent of tuning into the other person? In my formative years in learning and development I was subject to many training courses where I was encouraged to actively listen. This often included making notes, listening for the intent behind the words, giving non-verbal signals that I was listening and various other techniques. In isolation these aren't bad things to do, but they can get in the way of the purpose of listening – to fully understand what is being said. I have noticed a clear pattern in the most confident people that I work with. They are able to listen with an intensity which means that I can feel they are listening without them saying anything. I would highly recommend developing this talent. While it starts before the interaction that I mentioned earlier in the chapter, it requires a quieting of the mind while the other person is speaking. There will be times when you want to repeat back some of what they have said to clarify that you are receiving the message, but it is important to trust that focusing fully on them will lead you to be able to do this without making copious notes.

Exercise your ability to stay focused and connected with what they are saying until you are able to demonstrate that you are doing this without saying a word. The chances are you will know you are doing this brilliantly when people begin to give you praise and feedback on how brilliant a listener you are.

CONFIRM THEY MAKE SENSE

How do you demonstrate that you really understand where someone is coming from? How do you show that what they are saying makes sense? The most common way that I hear people demonstrating what they think is empathy is to tell a similar story about themselves as their partner in communication has told. This can often play out into conversation that feels semi-competitive. Person A shares a tale of the long hours they work and how their boss doesn't appreciate them. Person B says they know how they feel as they too are working exceptionally long hours, aren't appreciated by their boss and their partner is complaining that they don't see them. Person A then describes how it is going to get worse as the work is going to get busier and there is no more budget for extra staff. They will probably have to work 12-hour days every day just to keep on top of things. Person B agrees and says that that is the norm for them and they are now taking work home to do at the weekend. And so the conversation continues.

Now imagine if person B's first response was, 'Really, that must be tough. How do you manage to stay motivated when you are working that hard?' I am sure that you can see how this will change the dynamic of the conversation. It is a great demonstration of confidence to give the feeling that you know exactly where another person is coming from without making the conversation about you. This ability to relay information back or use phrases like 'that makes sense', 'I can understand why you might feel like that' or 'I can see where you are coming from' shows that you are not only listening but you appreciate their world view. Notice that it doesn't mean you share their world view. You can empathize with an individual's position without agreeing with them.

TAKE THE LIMELIGHT WHEN IT HELPS OTHERS

The ability and willingness to really hear others and give them the limelight is hugely valuable, but so is knowing when to step back into it. This understanding of when to step back in is something that highly confident people seem to develop naturally. If you haven't got to grips with this yet, then the key question is one of purpose. For example, if you are in a one-to-one conversation where someone is sharing the challenges in their relationship, ask yourself what is the purpose of them sharing this? If it is just to be heard, then the first two strategies in this chapter are likely to be enough. If you feel that they are engaging with you for advice and guidance, follow these two strategies, and then confidently step in with your ideas or experience.

In group situations the choice about when to step into the spotlight can still be made with the same purpose question. What is your purpose for being there and what is the others' purpose? If your purpose is connection with others in that meeting or at that event, then you will achieve that much more easily by focusing on the first two strategies in this chapter because people will perceive you as a good listener who understands them. If the purpose is to raise your profile or influence a decision then, while strategies one and two remain important, you need to be ready once you have stepped into their world to share your viewpoint or experience confidently.

Putting it all together

One of my most influential coaches once suggested to me that the only way to be truly confident is to first be completely vulnerable. While many people place vulnerability in the same category as weakness I experience it as the willingness to not always be right and being comfortable with imperfection. A differentiation between surface confidence or arrogance and deep genuine confidence is the ability to really listen and show genuine empathy without the ego getting in the way. For some of you this will be natural and the challenge will be the third strategy in this chapter, knowing when to step forward and shine in any particular situation. However, for many people reading this book, the challenge will come in feeling comfortable with in the first two strategies. When I train leaders in organizations in the art and magic of coaching, I find that the most common struggle for them is not to give their immediate answers and suggestions. When I work with professional footballers, those with the strength to focus on what is best for the dressing room and the team rather than act on what their ego is telling them are in the minority.

Many of the strategies contained in this book will help you to light up any room and shine in any situation. Practise these strategies until your natural in-built confidence radiates, but remember that this doesn't mean you always have to light up the room. The truly confident person knows that they can but that they don't have to.

9 Escape the prison of your beliefs

> *Just as no one can be forced into belief,*
> *so no one can be forced into unbelief.* Sigmund Freud

> *When one door closes, another opens: but we often look so*
> *long and so regretfully upon the closed door that we do not*
> *see the one which has opened for us.* Alexander Graham Bell

> *You see things; and you say, 'Why?'*
> *But I dream things that never were; and I say, 'Why not?'*
> George Bernard Shaw

> *I shut my eyes in order to see.* Paul Gauguin

> *Think left and think right and think low and think high.*
> *Oh, the thinks you can think up if only you try!* Dr Seuss

When I first started in the field of personal change, 'shifting
beliefs' was the thing to do. My first trainer in the field was pretty
obsessed by getting everyone he worked with to focus on
identifying, explaining and then working on deep-rooted personal
beliefs. Looking back now, it was a pretty problem-focused
approach to the subject (see Chapter 16 to learn more about
problem focus and solutions focus). I find the more you ask
people to explore their limiting beliefs the more limiting beliefs
they seem to notice or develop.

It is much more helpful to understand what beliefs are and where they come from. They then seem to be so much easier to move and sometimes just disappear without any real intervention.

Beliefs are simply stories that we learn or are taught about the world. If personal beliefs are an area you haven't explored before, the important part of the last sentence is 'stories'. Beliefs by nature are not true or fixed. In some cases these stories are repeated either by others to the point where they feel like they are real or absolute, but even most set beliefs held by one person will not be shared by others.

As human beings we are built to make meaning and build belief systems. What many in the self-development arena seem to forget is that we are also built to quickly change our beliefs. Most people in Western cultures will have believed in some version of Santa Claus as a child. If you did you will remember that every bit of evidence that you noted proved beyond doubt that he existed. The very moment that you knew he didn't everything changed and every piece of evidence demonstrated irrefutably that he didn't. Your beliefs changed and you noticed a different set of data.

Whether you are looking at your beliefs about yourself, your ability to do something or even your confidence itself, you don't need a complex neurological process to change them, you just need three steps:

1. See your beliefs for what they are.
2. Get evidence that disproves the belief.
3. Repeat.

BE AWARE OF YOUR BELIEFS

Beliefs are stories that we develop and hold onto that form rules and boundaries for our lives. They are largely unconscious; we often don't know why we can't do something or think that something is wrong for us, we *just do*.

Pause for a moment to think how your key beliefs developed. Usually parents will play a key role, as will our education. Our peer group will help shape them too alongside defining experiences that we regularly revisit. The more often we relive a particular belief the more real it will appear. It is not uncommon for a client to say, 'That's not a belief, that is a fact'. There are no real beliefs – just beliefs that seem real to you at specific times in your life.

Now would be a good time to examine the areas of your life that you would like more confidence in. What beliefs do you have about these areas that may be getting in the way of your confidence? Are these beliefs about you (someone like me couldn't do this), about your ability to do it (I'm not skilled/knowledgeable enough) or is it a belief about your confidence itself (I would be able to if only I was confident enough). Even just the process of seeing the focus of these beliefs will often take the energy out of them and make them seem less real.

TRY ON ALTERNATIVE BELIEFS

The structure of human experience is such that your beliefs will impact on what you do, how you do things and even your skills, knowledge and ability in certain situations. Put simply, your capability is dimmed down when your personal beliefs get in the way of your confidence. The flipside of this is that you can increase your ability and alter your normal behaviour by adopting some alternative beliefs.

Imagine that your confidence is low about an upcoming job interview because you believe that you don't create a good impression in formal interviews.

How will that affect how you act in the interview? How well formed will your answers be? How agile will your thinking be and how strong will the examples of your experience be?

Now consider what a more helpful belief would be. How would you prepare for the interview if you believed (or acted as if you believed) that you were brilliant in interviews? How would you walk into the interview? How would you sit? What would your voice be like? How would you respond to a challenging question? What would you say when the interviewer asked, 'Have you got any questions for us?'

Operating from different beliefs relies on the understanding that beliefs aren't real and that they can change. The good news is that you don't have to change a belief forever before you act as if it has changed. This will make perfect sense if you have read the earlier chapters about your brain's inability to differentiate between what is real and strongly imagined.

You can explore alternative beliefs and the impact that they will have on your capability and behaviour in any area of your life. Remember it is an experiment in changing your thinking. It may not feel immediately comfortable but it will help your brain to notice different data about what is true about you and the world you operate in, which will then help you to form new more helpful beliefs more easily.

JUST DO IT

The chances are that you are imagining the famous Nike swoosh and conjuring images of sports stars in their prime, but were these superstars always brilliant? Michael Jordan was the primary face of the company's advertising for many years and it was in a Nike ad that his most famous quote first appeared.

> I've missed more than 9000 shots in my career. I've lost almost 300 games. 26 times, I've been trusted to take the game winning shot and missed. I've failed over and over and over again in my life. And that is why I succeed. *Michael Jordan*

My invitation to you is not to wait until you are perfect before you test the limits of your self-belief. If your belief shows up as 'I can't' or 'I will never be able to', then why not just do it. If you don't have the confidence to write a book because you 'can't write', get a pen and paper and write a paragraph for the bin. If you 'couldn't ever' speak in front of a group', get your best friends together and ask them to listen to you while you stand and share a story from your favourite ever holiday. The aim is not to be the best writer or speaker in the world, but simply to disprove the limiting belief that will stop you ever developing your skills in this area.

Susan Jeffers explores this approach in great detail in the fantastic *Feel the Fear and Do it Anyway* (first published 1987). My favourite guideline from this book is: 'The only way to get rid of the fear of doing something is to go out and do it.' While it may not be the only way, I would agree that it is the quickest way. There is more on taking action later in this book.

Putting it all together

One of the key barriers to being at your confident best is your limiting beliefs. Understanding that your beliefs are neither universally true nor permanent is a brilliantly useful starting point for change. Beliefs should not be regarded as good or bad, but instead as helpful or not. While I would advocate developing an understanding of the beliefs that are getting in the way of your confidence, avoid deeply searching for limiting beliefs as you may just develop some that were not there before.

Highly confident people are very able to work around limiting beliefs about their abilities in certain situations. Some will explore other beliefs that may be more helpful to what they want to achieve, while others will simply act in spite of their beliefs.

Many people will see their beliefs as the bars to a prison of low confidence. The initial step is not to change their beliefs but to get them to understand that the prison only exists in their minds. When this kind of mental construct is created the only answer is to try and fight our way out. By developing an understanding that beliefs are just another type of thought you are thinking regularly, then it becomes easy to develop new beliefs or act in spite of them.

Perfect you

> **❝** You're lucky enough to be different, never change. Taylor Swift

> **❝** Labels are for filing. Labels are for clothing. Labels are not for people. Martina Navratilova

> **❝** You yourself, as much as anybody in the entire universe, deserve your love and affection. Buddha

> **❝** I think your whole life shows in your face and you should be proud of that. Lauren Bacall

> **❝** What I am is how I came out. No one's perfect and you just have to accept your flaws and learn to love yourself. Kelly Brook

A reflection on my school days has helped to crystallize my thoughts about the perfection or otherwise of human beings. I didn't have a terrible education, my schools were good and I was a decent student. Yet no matter how hard I tried or how well I performed there was always something else I was being told I should do better. At six years old I remember being told I was a silly, silly boy, at eight that I needed to try harder and at eleven I was informed that I would never amount to anything. I don't think that these were particularly bad teachers, but they are examples of a culture that sets us up to focus on and look for our imperfections.

Sadly this often continues into adulthood. As you can imagine I am a huge advocate of personal development, but this should never imply that you need fixing or are broken. Some approaches to therapy and psychology seem to imply the opposite. My absolute belief is that personal development is about making something wonderful even better. You are a diamond and applying the learning from this book simply helps to polish that diamond.

I always operate from a helpful belief that everyone has all of the resources they need to achieve what they want to achieve. That includes you. No matter what challenges you have faced during your life, they do not define you or limit what you can achieve. However difficult circumstances are for you, you are still fundamentally OK. You might not feel OK now and I am not invalidating or being dismissive of the scale of the problems that you or anyone else may face, but I think it is fundamentally unhelpful to think that you can't recover from these challenging times. You can recover, most people do and throughout any difficulties human beings remain fundamentally perfect

I am aware that while people feel out of touch with a sense of perfection, it is particularly difficult to trigger their state of confidence. That is what this chapter is designed to do, to help you focus on everything that is right with you and keep you connected with your ideal inner state.

I AM ALRIGHT

It's only right to start this section with a question from my coach and mentor and one of the greatest coaches on the planet, Michael Neill: 'How many babies do you know that are in therapy?'

Provided they are fed and watered, the human baby's natural state is one of wellbeing. I like to think of it as a state of being completely OK. Not OK in the British 'not too bad' sense, but instead one of perfection. Everything is completely OK.

This is a great place to start, but on the journey to feeling a genuine deep confidence it is even more powerful to realize that this state of wellbeing never leaves us. It is your default state and always there for you to access. You may not always be aware that it is there as life's challenges and your thinking about them get in the way of your connection with it but the core sense of 'I am alright' is alive in everyone.

I would encourage you to focus on this the next time your confidence seriously wavers. At the moment when a lack confidence creeps in, notice where in your body you actually do feel OK. You will find it somewhere and once you notice it there that sense of OK will start to spread through your body again.

FOCUS ON EVERYTHING THAT IS RIGHT WITH YOU

What is your best physical feature? How about your finest character trait? I would like to think that you could identify one of each, but if you were going list everything that is great about you how easy would you find it? Many people find it much easier to think about their flaws than their qualities and here-in lies a key confidence challenge. If you only notice what you perceive to be wrong with you, then confidence is never likely to be a state you remain in for long.

One of my favourite experiences of exploring this was with a professional footballer who had a reputation for being arrogant and difficult to manage. I asked him to list as many positive character traits as possible and all of the physical aspects that he was proud of. The lists were reasonably long but he hadn't realized that he had changed to listing negatives halfway through.

If focusing on everything that is right with you is a challenge now is a great time to make your list. Include both positive physical attributes and character traits. There are three things to look out for when you are completing this exercise:

1. How many attributes did you manage to list?
2. How comfortable did you find completing the exercise?
3. Is there anything on the list that surprised you?

Highly confident people don't write lists but they are just as comfortable in focusing on their positive characteristics and anything they want to improve.

AVOID PERFECTIONISM

Over the years I have arrived at the conclusion that perfectionism is a curse. I've worked with and coached many perfectionists and been married to one for over a decade! I am yet to meet one who enjoys their necessity for perfection.

The *Oxford English Dictionary* describes a perfectionist as 'a person who refuses to accept any standard short of perfection'. In other words, only 100 per cent right is right. The challenge is of course that life and the world aren't perfect. So to constantly strive for it will usually leave people feeling tired, disappointed and let down.

If this resonates with you, then working to reduce the desire for flawlessness will be incredibly useful. What in your life would it be useful to be less of a perfectionist in? Start with something simple that wouldn't matter to anyone but you (one of my clients took three months to get over the fact they weren't allowed to hang their clothes in order of both size and colour, so even this can be a challenge). Then work up to recognizing the positive traits in the imperfection of yourself and others.

I am not saying that highly confident people are sloppy, shoddy or are completely happy with their flaws and those of others. In some instances I appreciate perfectionism. I once was invited to work with a nuclear energy business and I really appreciated their obsession with perfection. However, I do also see the price perfectionists pay for their dedication to everything being just right. As well as the drag on energy the challenge in decision-making and the frustration with not being able to just get things done, it also damages confidence in many instances.

Putting it all together

One of the most challenging personal development exercises
I have ever been given was to look in the mirror every day
for a month and tell myself that I loved myself. I haven't
gone so far as to give you this exercise – it was particularly
stretching for me – but I do remember it triggering a
useful train of thoughts about just what there was for me
to love about me. All too often others will point out our
imperfections and all too often we will then continue to
focus on those imperfections while forgetting about the
positive attributes.

It is this kind of thinking that clouds our connection with our
default state. This state of being blissfully OK stays with us
throughout our lives. No matter how things are in life you
are fundamentally perfect as you are. While self-improvement
is a good thing, especially the building of a constant and
consistent state of confidence, this doesn't mean that you are
in any way lacking. It simply shows that you have the ability
to make your amazing self even better.

The detail of your confidence

❝ *If you're presenting yourself with confidence, you can pull off pretty much anything.* Katy Perry

❝ *I was always looking outside myself for strength and confidence but it comes from within. It is there all the time.* Anna Freud

❝ *I think the best way to have confidence is not to allow everyone else's insecurities to be your own.* Jessie J.

❝ *People wrote me off, but I believed in myself.
I got the confidence back, and it grew and grew.
I won my first major and my last at the place that changed my life.* Pete Sampras

❝ *On a scale of one to ten, I'd rate my body confidence as a good seven. Everyone has their hang-ups, but I see my body as a training tool and I feel good about it.* Jessica Ennis-Hill

If by now you aren't crystal clear in your understanding that confidence is a state, then I'd recommend that you go back to the start and read Chapter 1 again. This fundamental understanding really is the foundation of mastering your confidence.

Having a deeper awareness of what your confidence is like will put you on the fast track to self-assurance whenever you need it. This chapter will help you to become really familiar with the component parts of your personal version of the state of confidence and how it shows up in your body and mind.

For a moment, I would like you to focus on your memories. I am certain, because of my understanding of the brain, that if you think of your most powerful memory it will be a rich and multi-faceted memory. It will have detail to it and you are likely to experience that memory in all of the senses – even though it is just in your head. In order for memories to be strong they must be multi-sensory when they are created. In exploring and understanding this detail and how it aligns to your mental states you can understand more about your confidence.

To prepare for the rest of this chapter I would like you to revisit a specific memory. I would like you to think about your favourite holiday ever. Now go to a specific time or moment from that holiday. Focus on the memory for a moment. Notice the pictures that you are making in your head. What are the colours like? Are they bright or dull? Are the pictures moving or still? Do they have a frame around them or do they surround you? What else do you notice when you focus on the pictures?

Now notice the sounds in the memory. Where in your head do you hear the sounds? In front of you, behind you, to the side or all around? Notice the volume, pitch and tone of the sounds.

Finally notice the feelings that this memory has generated. Where in your body are you noticing the feelings? Be really specific. What direction does it seem that the feelings are moving? Do the feelings have a texture or temperature?

The ability to notice feelings in this detail will help you to understand your confidence more than ever before.

EXPLORE YOUR DETAIL DIFFERENCES

In order to quickly understand the differences between your sensory focus when you are confident compared to when you aren't, try this experiment. It will be most effective if you can familiarize yourself with the questions, then close your eyes when doing each part of the exploration.

Think of an event in the past when you felt less than confident. Really associate into it, and see it through your own eyes, as if it were happening now. Notice what the pictures are like:

- Are they moving or still?
- How successful are you seeing yourself being?
- What are the colours, contrast and brightness like?

Now focus on the sounds.

- What kinds of things are you hearing? Are they supportive or not?
- Notice the volume and pitch of what you can hear.
- Also notice where the sounds are coming from.

Finally take notice of what feelings this has generated in you.

- Are they familiar?
- What would you label them as?
- Where specifically in the body are they?
- Are they moving or still? Do they have a shape?

Having noticed the pictures, sounds and feelings that you were focusing on, change your physiology completely for a moment before moving onto the second part. Stand up and move around, even sitting in a different position will help. When you've shaken off the feeling of unconfident, then you're ready to move on to the next part.

Now think of an event in the past in which you felt supremely confident. Again associate into it, see it through your own eyes, as if it were happening now.

Now notice what the pictures are like.

- Are they moving or still?
- How successful are you seeing yourself being?
- What are the colours, contrast and brightness like?

Again move onto the sounds.

- What kinds of things are you hearing? Are they support- ive now?
- Notice the volume and pitch of what you can hear.
- Also notice where the sounds are coming from.

Now take notice of what feelings this has generated in you.

- Are they familiar?
- What would you label them as?
- Where specifically in the body are they?
- Are they moving or still? Do they have a shape?

You will have quickly noticed some specific differences in the sensory detail between confident and unconfident. When I first worked with a professional footballer using this framework he quickly found himself running a number of negative 'strategies'. His internal pictures were all of the situation going badly. He was performing poorly and others were showing a much higher level of ability. His internal dialogue had switched to negative and critical, he was hearing himself complain, and imagining his manager pointing out his weaknesses. Finally he had a significant knot in his stomach – no surprise bearing in mind what he was focusing on!

I then had him focus on the experience that he had full confidence in. Within seconds his internal pictures had changed. In addition to the internal pictures now showing success and the whole scenario going well, they were also brighter and clearer; mentally it was a sunny day! The auditory tape had changed too; now his internal dialogue was positive and supportive as was the imagined language of those around him. Finally, and most interestingly for me, the knot had moved. Rather than the intense feeling in his stomach, it was now an equally intense feeling in his chest – the same one he gets whenever he is excited!

USE THE DETAIL FOR INSTANT CONFIDENCE

This client found his key focus differences for fear and excitement and confident and unconfident. The differences between the two will vary from person to person, but what remains the same is your ability to change the focus.

This is a great time to remember that the brain does not differentiate time easily. The same neural networks are fired up when we remember a time from the past and when we imagine a time in the future. This ambiguity in the brain means that we can apply the learning from this chapter in three ways:

1. **In the moment.** If you notice that you are running your unconfident sensory programmes, then you can change them. In the example of the footballer this would include imagining the sun shining brighter, some really positive self-talk and making sure that

knot moved from his stomach up to his chest to
trigger his feeling of confidence and excitement.

2. **To feel at your brilliantly confident best about future events.** When you think about a situation in the future, which set of strategies do you notice kicking in? By ensuring you are seeing, hearing and feeling the event in the detail of your confidence, you are dramatically increasing the likelihood of being confident when the time comes.

3. **To change how you feel about events from the past.** If you take an event from the past and change the details of that memory to those that would be triggered in a confident memory, then you can begin changing how that memory is stored and its emotional impact. This is particularly useful and worth practising if you have a specific memory that consistently impacts on your overall confidence.

SPIN YOUR FEELINGS

There is one additional technique that can help change the detail of your state of confidence in seconds. Some years ago when I began studying modern psychologies, I observed a couple of leaders in the field of Neuro-Lingustic Programming helping clients to spin their feelings to great effect.

This involved the person being coached in identifying the direction that a feeling was moving in their body and changing its direction to influence the emotional state connected to it.

Try this on the feeling you associated with the less confident memory from the earlier experiment. When you notice which way the feeling is moving imagine gently slowing it down and then getting it to move in the opposite direction. As you do this you'll notice a different, more useful state being triggered. If you practise this ahead of time you will also be able to do it live as you approach challenging situations and no one else will ever know.

Putting it all together

Every state that we experience has its own detail. Our internal pictures will have different degrees of clarity, movement and intensity. Sounds will appear in different places around our heads and change in volume tone and cadence. Feelings will appear to move differently through the body starting in different places and have different textures. By building our awareness of the detail of our confidence we can learn to master it as a state to access and intensify at any moment. We can switch quickly away from a lack of confidence and even change our experience of an event from the past. While this requires some time, attention and practice, the benefits are huge especially if confidence has been a long-term issue and prior to reading this book you thought that it would take some outside influence to build it. I would also particularly recommend mastering this practice if confidence directly affects your performance in your job. I have coached professional athletes, performers and public speakers through the process with huge rewards.

12 Confidence comes from calm

❝ *Be like a duck. Calm on the surface, but always paddling like the dickens underneath.* Michael Caine

❝ *He who is of calm and happy nature will hardly feel the pressure of age, but to him who is of an opposite disposition youth and age are equally a burden.* Plato

❝ *Panic causes tunnel vision. Calm acceptance of danger allows us to more easily assess the situation and see the options.* Simon Sinek

❝ *Turn off your mind, relax, and float downstream.* John Lennon

❝ *Work. Don't Think. Relax.* Ray Bradbury

It is fascinating to see the reactions of those I work with to the notion of relaxing. In the late 20th century relaxation in the Western world was often seen as the domain of those with hippie tendencies. While there is a greater acceptance in the 21st century of the benefits of purposeful relaxing most still see it as an extra-curricular lack of activity to fit around normal life.

If this sounds familiar to you, a quick examination of relaxing should reset your attitudes and move you to slowing down in more areas of your life.

I want to make clear that being pro-calm doesn't mean being anti-busy or even anti-fast. The thought that calm and quick are opposites is a result of the 20th-century view of calm. Dictionary antonyms of calm include *frenzied, turbulent, violent* and *wild*. It's possible to be energetic and calm. My family have been involved in the RNLI for most of their lives and I have seen my eldest brother working in the gravest of emergency situations at sea. He is completely focused with a sense of calm but with absolute urgency.

This chapter shares tips to restore calmness and to relax without having to retreat under a tree for days to meditate. I see relaxation and calmness as siblings from the same family. Relaxation generally has a slower pace to it. Both have health benefits in their combating the impact of stress-related issues such as sleep and eating disorders, problems with the skin and longer term health issues affecting the heart. All of these will inhibit your confidence. By practising the tips in this chapter you will see other positive results too. You are likely to find yourself thinking more clearly and remaining more rational when under pressure.

I would recommend reading this chapter in an environment where you can experiment with the tips given here quickly. Ideally this would be in a fairly quiet private space. If this isn't possible the first time you read it, then be sure to revisit another time when you can.

BREATHE CALMLY

Some years ago I attended a workshop on breaking through mental barriers in business. All was going well until the facilitator suggested that the group of around 100 people learn some breathing techniques. I associated this method of relaxation with weekend retreats rather than business programmes. I was very wrong.

This simple technique helps me to sleep when travelling and to prepare for large presentations. I have used it to calm myself before I settled my baby to sleep and to get ready for some very tough one-to-one conversations. Clients have credited this technique with increasing their run rate (cricketers), having more energy during games (footballers) and being able to face a barrage of questions from a tyrannical managing director. Best of all it is short and very easy.

Get ready by sitting in a chair, in a position that is comfortable for you, with both feet flat on the floor. When you are comfortable follow this process:

1. Breathe in for your own count of eight.
2. Hold the breath in for your own count of eight.
3. Breathe out for your own count of eight. Make sure you breathe all of the air out; you might need to 'push' it out.
4. Hold, with no air in for your own count of four.
5. Repeat steps 1—4 twice more.

That is the whole technique! It is very simple and very powerful.

You will find the more you practise, the calmer it will help you to be. I find it even more powerful if I can close my eyes when I am going through the 8-8-8-4 process, but if that isn't possible then focus on the breathing pattern.

Here are just a few examples of situations where it will help:

- Before a presentation. It will relax you and help regulate your breathing to allow you to deliver the presentation more effectively and powerfully.
- Whenever you feel overwhelmed.
- Before you start a key task to help you focus and work more effectively.
- Before you exercise.
- To relax at the end of the day.
- To prepare for a difficult discussion or meeting at home or work.
- Any other time it would be useful to be focused and relaxed.

USE MUSIC TO RELAX

How does music impact on your mood? My guess is that you have a piece of music that, if you hear it, automatically lifts your mood and energy levels. But do you have a piece of music that automatically relaxes and calms you? Music has a huge impact on our biology. In simple terms, our brainwave patterns and heart rate will align with the beats per minute of any piece of music we are listening to. This is known as entrainment. While musical preference can be a factor, it is important to know that you don't have to love a piece of music for it to have a relaxing effect on you. Baroque music and, more specifically, music with a tempo of 60 beats per minute, has long been considered to be ideal for inducing relaxing states. Scientists in Manchester, England, recently claimed to have made the most relaxing tune in history. The song, called 'Weightless' and compiled by Marconi Unicorn, induced a deeper state of relaxation than any other they tested.

I would highly recommend creating your own relaxation playlist. Technology can really help us with this. You can make technically fantastic relaxation playlists by searching for music with a bpm of 60. A quick Google search will provide you with a huge choice. You can also use a music download system like iTunes or Amazon to create a specific playlist for your mp3 or mp4 player. If you do have strong musical preferences then I would recommend that you keep your selection quite neutral although there are more contemporary tunes that can be relaxing, these include 'Mellomaniac' (Chill Out Mix) by DJ Shah, 'Watermark' by Enya, 'We Can Fly' by Café Del Mar and 'Airstream' by Electra.

SWITCH STUFF OFF

The final relaxation strategy in this chapter is very practical but usually completely overlooked in the modern world in which we live. We live in the most stimulated environment in history. Multitasking is the norm. There are evenings where I have found myself watching television while reading emails on my laptop and posting on social media on my telephone. I have clients for whom this is the norm yet they wonder why they find it a challenge to relax.

Research has shown that night time light exposure suppresses the production of melatonin which is the major hormone that controls sleep and wake cycles. A suppression of melatonin can also have longer reaching impacts on your weight, heart and immune system. The type of light typically emitted by devices such as iPhones, tablets, LCD televisions and computer screens is close to the peak sensitivity of melatonin suppression. Add this science to the fact that when we are looking at tablets, smartphones or computers it is typically to engage in things that will stimulate our brains and even our relaxing TV watching will usually be a stimulating drama or comedy, so it is easy to see that we are making real relaxation difficult.

So the strategy is simple. Switch it off. We are a generation that has forgotten that switching off a mobile device does not mean we miss things; it means that we can get to it another time. Many people have the capacity to record their favourite television drama, yet feel the need to stay up and watch it.

Essentially I am saying that you should put yourself back in control of your choices and be aware of what really works for you and what doesn't. If you find it a challenge to relax, then try switching off your technology earlier and taking a relaxing bath and notice the difference.

Putting it all together

Confidence rarely looks rushed. Even at times of challenge the highly confident person appears composed. They are able to be fully activated, aware and alert when required and able to relax, switch off and are calm when the time is right. We live in a world where busy is the norm and you may be one of many people who find it challenging to take your foot off the proverbial gas. The ability to relax, though, is a desirable attribute and if you regularly find yourself stressed or over-activated for the task at hand or the environment that you are in, then I would highly recommend that you use this chapter to begin the journey to make calm a state that you are in more of the time. Confidence is a state that requires clear thinking and the ninety miles an hour mind-chatter of a person who is always on full and struggles to sleep are rarely a good mix. So when would be a good time to start to relax?

13 Innate confidence

“ *You can't connect the dots looking forward, you can only connect them looking backwards. So you have to trust that the dots will somehow connect in your future. You have to trust in something: your gut, destiny, life, karma, whatever. Because believing that the dots will connect down the road will give you the confidence to follow your heart, even when it leads you off the well-worn path.* Steve Jobs

“ *There have been so many people who have said to me, 'You can't do that,' but I've had an innate belief that they were wrong. Be unwavering and relentless in your approach.* Halle Berry

“ *I was always looking outside myself for strength and confidence, but it comes from within. It is there all the time.* Anna Freud

“ *The intuitive mind is a sacred gift and the rational mind is a faithful servant. We have created a society that honours the servant and has forgotten the gift.* Albert Einstein

“ *Instinct is untaught ability.* Bain

Have you ever wondered how tiny seeds can grow into huge trees that last thousands of years? I don't mean the process of converting food and light but how that tree knows it needs to do that? How does an acorn know how to grow into an oak rather than a pine? How does your mouth know when to water? I know why we sweat, but not how my body learned to do it. I have never had to force my body to do it; it just does. Even the simplest of processes like blinking. Have you ever considered how the eyelids of a tiny baby know how to do this at just the right time and at just the right pace?

When you consider these small and seemingly insignificant examples, it begins to become apparent there is some kind of intelligence to the universe and to us as human beings. Most people agree that there is some kind of greater force at play. Some think it is a spiritual one, some call it nature, others believe in a range of forces that control the flow of our life and destiny.

What I am sure of is that you, like everyone else, have an innate intelligence and confidence that does its best to take care of you. I am pretty sure that you have never had to concentrate on a cut to make it heal. Over time it just will. If you are a mother, the fear of having a child must at some point have been overridden by the confidence that you could do it.

The realization that this innate intelligence is alive in you and everyone and everything around you will play a huge part in cementing your confidence. When you listen calmly enough and well enough to what your intuition is saying you will always do the right thing. This chapter aims to help you to hear that still small voice within more of the time, but first, if you still doubt your innate intelligence please pause for a moment and pay attention to your breathing.

How do you know how to do that?

CONNECT WITH YOUR INTELLIGENCE

One of the defining factors in the most confident people I work with is that they are easily able to tell the difference between the type of mind-chatter that runs around our heads whenever there is pressure, or a decision, to be made and their real intelligence. Learning this distinction is a huge step to securing your genuine long-term confidence.

If you aren't easily aware of this intuitive voice or feeling, then take the first step now to try to connect with it.

    1. Sit comfortably in your seat or lie comfortably in your bed.

2. Place the book somewhere that you can read it with out holding it.
3. Notice any chatter that is going on in your mind. Pay attention to the pitch, pace and tone of that internal voice.
4. Now become aware of your breathing. For a minute or so just pay attention to its gentle rise and fall.
5. Notice the sensations of your body against your chair or bed, for example the feeling of your arms against the arms of chair or the backs of your legs touching your bed.
6. Become aware of the feeling of blinking as it happens.
7. Spend another moment experiencing these newly noticed sensations.
8. Now notice how you are noticing them. Beyond any mind-chatter that is still there and beyond your body's physical connection with the environment you have an awareness of yourself. Pay attention to it. Notice what that is like for you.

Even the most sceptical clients that I take through this exercise get a pleasant surprise when they notice the first step to a real connection with the intelligence that has guided you through the best times of your life.

PUT YOUR INNATE INTELLIGENCE INTO ACTION

Think of a decision that you have been wrestling with for some time. Why have you found it hard to move forward with it? My guess is that your internal chatter has got in the way of your more intelligent self. Having just completed the previous exercise you may already have a clearer idea of the next step. If not run through the exercise again and when you reach the final step of the process ask yourself the question, 'What is the best next step?' Notice what occurs to you, not from the mind-chatter but from the other awareness.

This isn't to say that every time you have a decision to make that you have to stop and relax into a chair. I am simply helping you to make a distinction that the highly confident seem to do easily. When you connect more readily to your innate intelligence you are able to make better decisions and take better actions.

The next time you are in a challenging situation with your family, pay attention to your more intelligent self, ignoring the mind-chatter that inevitably starts in these situations. Act based on that intuitive voice and notice the difference in your response and the impact on the situation.

In challenging business meetings listen past the mind-talk that can confuse or ignite situations for the stiller guide that will help you make a more valuable contribution. It is not always easy, especially if you haven't been aware of it before, but it is always valuable for you and others.

SEE THE INTELLIGENCE OF OTHERS

You will have people in your life who always seem to be at their most intelligent best. They always seem to know the right thing to do and are at ease making even the biggest decisions.

Then there will be others around you who don't seem to have connected with their more intelligent self for some time. They often make bad decisions or do the wrong thing even when the right thing seems blindingly obvious to everyone around them. You may find it difficult to believe they have an intuition that guides them, and it may seem like the indelible intelligence of the universe has passed them by.

As your confidence and innate intelligence grow you may find that connecting with these people becomes an increasing challenge. This is a particular issue if this person is a family member, work colleague or client. Here are three additional steps to help you be at your best around these people and even help them to tune into their intuition.

See their positive intent

Every behaviour has or once had a positive intent. It serves a purpose to that person even if we believe that purpose is misguided. For example the positive intention behind aggressive behaviour is often protection. The positive intention or purpose behind fear is usually safety. By seeing the positive intent behind behaviour we can deal with behaviour more resourcefully.

See them at their best

It is possible that you are only seeing this person when they are at their worst. In busy day-to-day life partners can see each other as they wake and pull themselves around for the day ahead and when they return home from long challenging days at work. You are likely to have work colleagues who you only meet in difficult business meetings.

Take the time to connect with people when they have the opportunities to be at their best. This may be at different times of the day or in different environments.

Feedback on the positive

Take the time to let them know specifically when you have seen them at their best. Give feedback on positive behaviours or when you think their decisions or actions have had a positive impact. This could be just the trigger they need to understand what they do when they are at their best and to do more of it. They will appreciate you more too.

Putting it all together

In the book *Big Mind Big Heart,* Zen master Dennis Genpo Merzel says: 'There is a transcendent awareness, a Big Mind, a Big Heart, present and readily accessible to each and everyone of us. When we realize it, we see it is the source of true peace, happiness, satisfaction, courage and joy.' It is this awareness that I want to connect clients with. While peace, happiness, satisfaction, courage and joy are the most noble of pursuits I want every reader to use this intelligence to make a difference to their day-to-day, moment-by-moment activities. Connecting with your most intelligent self leads to better relationships, more successful businesses and healthier lives.

This is in no way a fluffy topic; a reader who sees this as 'tree-huggy' is missing the practical impact of being connected to the same intelligence that quite literally makes the world go around. Your innate intelligence feeds your confidence and I believe the reverse is also true. The truly confident person is more easily able to pay attention to their smartest self. This is a most amazing loop to be going around where your intuition feeds your confidence and your confidence connects you more readily with what Gandhi called your 'still small voice within'.

14 Get more of what you focus on

CC *Optimism is the faith that leads to achievement. Nothing can be done without hope and confidence.* Helen Keller

CC *Our way of thinking creates good or bad outcomes.* Stephen Richards

CC *We are what we think...*
All that we are, arises with our thoughts.
With our thoughts we make our world. Buddha

CC *Yes We Can!* Barack Obama

CC *When things go wrong, don't go with them.* Elvis Presley

I'd like to start this chapter with three quick mental exercises. If it is safe to do so, stop what you are doing for a few minutes and reflect on the last 24 hours. Ask yourself the question, 'How did I do'? With no other particular criteria, just a simple review of the last day and night, how was it and how were you?

Now for a further moment, reflect on your reflections. Did you notice more of what went well or what didn't? Did you see more of the things you did well, no matter how big or small, or the things that didn't go as you would have liked?

Finally for now I would like you to cast your mind forward over the next 24 hours or so. Think about the things you will be doing. Run them through your head as if they were happening now. Notice again whether things are generally going well or badly and how you are imagining yourself doing in these situations.

Unless you are an unusually positive and confident person you are likely to have noticed some good and some bad, but it is important to be aware of where you placed the emphasis. If you noticed more things going badly and your role in those things happening, you will be negatively impacting on your confidence.

There is an important fact about the brain that those rich in confidence know and tap into to help maintain and grow that precious state.

The brain is built to follow commands that it is given.

When we focus on some data the brain will take this as a directive to find more evidence or information to prove that data to be true. When applied specifically to confidence, this means that the brain will search for more examples of what you focus on most. If in your reflection at the beginning of this chapter you thought most about the things that didn't go well and in particular your role in them, the likelihood is that your brain is currently paying more attention to situations that will negatively affect your confidence. It will also be filtering out some positive experiences that would help build your confidence.

FILTERING IN POSITIVE EXPERIENCES

Various research suggests that the brain processes a huge amount of data every second. I have seen estimates of between 20 million and 400 billion pieces of information being processed every second. However, we are only consciously aware of a small portion of these processes. The most reliable research that I am aware of suggests an awareness of around 20 pieces of information every second. Our brains are designed to filter out a huge amount of data so there are memories and live experiences that we are never aware of. People who are confident tend to notice and remember more experiences that are positive and affirming, while one of the challenges of being low on confidence is that the brain provides more data to sustain that state.

This gives more evidence to support the idea that a conscious routine of noticing what has gone well on a day-to-day basis will create a solid platform for confidence. The process of doing this will help us into that state on a more regular basis and will also help to programme the brain to notice more of the positive actions and results, which in turn will further grow our confidence.

CONNECT THE PAST, THE PRESENT AND THE FUTURE

Without being a neuroscientist you know that reflecting on certain memories triggers certain emotions. You will also be aware that your thoughts about live situations trigger certain emotions too. I am certain that at some point you have imagined yourself in a particular situation in the future with certain emotions being triggered.

When you realize that you have done this naturally it becomes unsurprising to learn that the brain does not differentiate between imagination, memory and current experience. When you remember a situation in the past when you were confident exactly the same neuro-wiring is used as when you imagine yourself being hugely confident. When you feel confident in the moment, that same wiring is activated. This knowledge is wonderfully useful in thinking your world to life. You get the same confidence boost from imagining yourself doing something confidently, as you do when you remember yourself doing something confidently.

The brain connects the activity and the feeling that you have as if it actually happened. This means a neural pathway connecting your physical ability to do whatever the activity is and the state of confidence already exists. When you come to do it you will automatically feel confident.

Practise mentally rehearsing. Regularly see, hear and feel yourself doing things confidently to create the pathway more deeply. When you do the activity and feel confident, this will reinforce it even further and even more strongly, but, you don't need to wait until the first time you do something to create the state of your confidence in the brain connected with that activity.

REHEARSE THE RIGHT PHYSIOLOGY

Candice Pert is a Nobel-nominated neuroscientist and her work has been core to my understanding of the impact of our thinking on the body and its physiology. Dr Pert is often quoted as saying 'the brain is located within and throughout the body'. Her ground-breaking work, captured in *Molecules of Emotion*, confirmed what many social psychologists and modern therapists had known for sometime – that your brain programmes your body. There are numerous sporting studies that underline the fact that mental rehearsal does even more than create states and memory paths to help you function well and confidently in certain situations. Put simply, this mental preparation programmes your physiology ahead of time.

Let's apply this to a situation that many people feel they need more confidence in – presenting to large audiences. From this chapter so far you will already know that remembering a time when you have done something similar and imagining your presentation in detail will help you feel confident and be mentally prepared. You can now be sure that by seeing yourself walking on to the stage with a straight posture and steady strides will programme your muscles and increase the likelihood of your maintaining this physiology. The mental rehearsal of hearing your voice steady, calm and powerful will again trigger an internal reaction that primes your vocal apparatus to do exactly this. Throughout the book you will learn even more about the impact your physiology has on the chemistry of your brain, but for now you can be sure that mental practice impacts significantly on your body's performance.

Putting it all together

Thinking your world to life means more than a bit of visualization. It is a way to become the pilot and the plane of your confidence. A combination of mental rehearsal of confidence in situations and detailed mental review of confident times from the past will do three crucial things:

1. Create a connection in your brain between what you want to do and the state of confidence.

2. Programme your brain to filter in more examples of you at your confident best and notice less examples of confidence lacking.
3. Prepare you physiologically for a confident experience.

The great news is that you don't have to spend hours and hours to create this programming. My experience is that short, focused sessions are better than long-winded visualizations. In fact most clients I work with report that five minutes a day just after they have woken up or when they are settling down for sleep has the biggest impact. It is important to do this thinking as if you were in the situation, seeing it through your own eyes, rather than watching yourself in the situation, as if on a TV screen. In fact this is a secret of confidence in itself. Confident people tend to see themselves performing well in an associated way (through their own eyes) and performing badly in a disassociated way (as if they were watching themselves from a distance). People who find confidence difficult to experience often have the opposite pattern. Now is a great time to ensure that your pattern is that of the confident person you are becoming.

15 Create a confident future

> *To reach a port, we must sail – Sail, not tie at anchor – Sail, not drift.* Franklin D. Roosevelt

> *It is good to have an end to journey toward; but it is the journey that matters, in the end.* Ernest Hemingway

> *Far away there in the sunshine are my highest aspirations. I may not reach them, but I can look up and see their beauty, believe in them, and try to follow where they lead.* Louisa May Alcott

> *If you were born without wings, do nothing to prevent them from growing.* Coco Chanel

> *An aim in life is the only fortune worth finding.* Robert Louis Stevenson

Before you start this chapter, make sure that you have something to write with close to hand. You are about to discover a simple but powerful tool that will significantly increase the chances of bringing any life goals to life. Whether you are working on confidence in a specific area or your confidence overall, this small shift in how you set goals and talk about the future will make a big difference.

Before I explain it in more detail, it's useful to do the following quick exercise. Choose one area of your life and write down four or five goals that would be great to achieve in that area. For example:

Life area – health and fitness:

- Lose 10 lbs.
- Exercise for 20 minutes three times a week.
- Drink 2 litres of water every day.
- Cut out processed carbs for two weeks every month.

Now write the same list but in the present tense, as if it has happened already.

Life area – health and fitness:

- I have lost 10 lbs.
- I exercise for 20 minutes three times a week, every week.
- I am fully hydrated. I drink 2 litres of water every day.
- For two weeks every month I eat completely clean, cutting out all processed food.

Review your two lists. Even though I have asked you to do this as a quick exercise, notice which list gives you more energy. Notice which list gives you the greater feeling of motivation and which list triggers more ideas of which actions to take.

There is something powerful in creating goals and aspirations in the present tense. Despite the brain's inability to differentiate well between the tenses it does react more strongly to the immediate. It will search more quickly for more data relating to a goal that is created as if it is happening now. A goal written in this tense will feel closer or more realistic. I often notice a physiological difference in clients' reactions to their goals when written in the present tense. When goals are written in the future I see clients shuffling, shaking their heads or squinting as they struggle to work out how they are going to achieve it. When the same client talks about the same goals in the present tense I see them moving forward, smiling and a small quickening in pace or movement; all from a change in tense.

YOUR CONFIDENT FUTURE HISTORY

The future history exercise is one that is brilliant and spooky. Many of the most confident and most successful people that I know use the exercise to set the scene for the year ahead in their career or life. One professional footballer credited this process as the main reason he got a £2 million transfer to a Premier League club in England.

The best thing is that the process works. The second best thing is that it is super simple. Choose a point in time in the future that is appropriate for you to set goals to. Somewhere between a year and eighteen months seems to work best for most people I work with. It is most useful to choose a specific date. It is also helpful to choose somewhere you would love to be on that date in the future. Somewhere that you love being at that time of year is best. Now choose someone in your life that you could write a letter to about what you've achieved in your life. It is useful for it to be someone significant but not someone who triggers any sort of negative emotion or embarrassment. It is worth noting that you aren't actually going to send the letter, it is simply useful for the process to have someone to write it to. If you can't think of anyone, write the letter to yourself. Now imagine you are able to fast-forward through time to that date and answer this question:

Imagine it is (your date) and you are the most confident version of yourself that you could ever have imagined being. As you sit (in your chosen place) relaxing, you realize that this genuine and almost permanent sense of confidence has positively impacted on every area of your life, including family, health, your financial situation, work and every other area of your life you can imagine. Write a letter to (your chosen person) describing your life as it is now in as much rich detail as possible. Also include some of the major milestones over the last year or so that have brought you to where you are now.

DREAM BOARDS

A development of this process is to create your future history in a visual format that you can refer to consistently. For most adults it will have been many years since you created a montage of any sort, but this is a perfect opportunity to revisit your childhood in pursuit of real confidence. As with the previous process it is useful to have a specific point in the future your dream board is created for. Then as you imagine the impact of being your most confident self, create a montage of the key ways that this will manifest. Make the dream board as a rich and engaging as possible. This is not the time to be overly logical or reserved in any way.

I know some families who create dream boards together at the beginning of a new year as a way to cement a shared set of goals for the future. Children will be even less restrained and often set even more aspirational targets; in this process that's no bad thing!

It is important to have your dream board displayed somewhere that you will see it regularly. One personal development guru recommends having it under your pillow and looking at it every morning and evening in the transition between waking and sleeping states. I prefer to have it somewhere that I will see it regularly and unconsciously. I know that my brain will continue to process the data even if I am not aware of it.

PLANNING BACKWARDS

In both the previous strategies in this chapter, we are relying on the brain to unconsciously use these aspirational goals to guide our actions towards achieving them without realizing and there is no doubt that they work for many people. If you want to be even surer of achieving your confident future then create an action plan to bring your confident future history to life. One of the challenges of action planning for many people is that the very creation of the initial small steps towards this huge end goal can in itself demotivate by presenting a stark reminder of how far you have to go.

There is an alternative process for goal setting that can in itself motivate and energize as well as helping you to find creative ways to achieve your goals.

Take one of the elements of the future history that you created in part one of this chapter.

> 1. Ask yourself this question: 'What was the very last step that I took just before I achieved this goal?' It may take some time to answer this at first but when you have the answer write it down.

2. Now as you think of that answer, ask the question: 'What was the very last step that happened just before this?'
3. As you answer this, ask: 'And the step before that?

Continue the process until you have worked your way back to the starting point. You will have created a whole action plan in reverse order and it will be fuller and more energizing than it would have been if you had created it in the traditional way. If you currently action plan forwards as part of your work, then this reverse process can feel a little counterintuitive; however, with a little practice you may even change how you plan your work process too.

Putting it all together

The brain is an amazing organ that we are only really just beginning to understand. One of the few things that the brain does not do well is distinguish between time frames and tenses. Exploitation of this small loophole can fast-track your journey to genuine and consistent confidence.

Highly confident people or those on the journey to becoming confident can create rich aspirational goals for the future but expressed in the present tense to positively confuse the brain's understanding of how close we are to that goal. The process of creating these future histories, whether in words or pictures, is energizing and motivating in itself.

These future histories can be supported by the creation of action plans – created from the furthest point in the future backwards in time – which will all but guarantee that what can seem like a fantasy when first created will become reality in the most natural way.

16 Make personal development a must

> **Absorb what is useful, discard what is not, add what is uniquely your own.** Bruce Lee

> **We must become the change we want to see.** Mahatma Gandhi

> **Life isn't about finding yourself. Life is about creating yourself.** George Bernard Shaw

> **What we think, we become.** Buddha

> **The only journey is the journey within.** Rainer Maria Rilke

My study of the subject of confidence over the last ten years has brought me together with many wonderful people. There are few who I have learned more from and with than Steve Marriott. Steve coaches with razor-sharp precision and works with clients using a powerfully persuasive style that leaves them with no choice but to do the right thing. In this chapter Steve defines beautifully why personal development is a must and shares his strategies for doing it perfectly.

I failed.

I graduated from school in the 5 per cent of my class who made the top 95 per cent look good, and with an A-star in low confidence. If it wasn't enough that I'd 'failed', I compounded my confidence issues by continually valuing everyone else's expertise and authority above my own.

Determined to change this I embarked upon a self-improvement mission and soon found myself regularly trawling the shelves of business and self-help texts as well as following the crowd to every seminar spouting the 'latest' model and method. I learned some fantastic and helpful things. I also wasted a huge amount of time, money and effort on a lot of less useful 'development' fads. My intention in this chapter is to spare you from the dark side of development and show you three ways to make your personal development a must.

So before we begin let me offer you my own definition of 'personal development'.

Personal development should never be the endless acquisition of more and more information. Information in and of itself is relatively useless. Real personal development is all about action; your ongoing development should inspire you to think differently and more creatively, understand yourself and others more deeply, challenge your status quo and ultimately have an impact in your own life as well as the lives of others. If that isn't a recipe for confidence, I don't know what is.

Audacious? I hope so. Scary? Perhaps a little, but in a good way.

I believe personal development is a contact sport, and one that pays dividends to those who play full-out. That's not to say you should attend every seminar, high-fiving and 'Hell Yeah'-ing, and read every book as the unquestionable truth.

The 'what' you choose to develop and how is entirely your choice; whatever your preference my advice is to fully commit to it and apply your whole self to the learning.

A word of caution … in our world of immediate reward, everyone is looking for the 'fast track' to success. I haven't discovered a magic pill to personal development but here are my strategies to make the journey more fun and help you along the way.

START WITH 'WHY?'

No this isn't a trick question. The biggest reason personal development of any kind fails is because a clear and compelling 'why' hasn't been established. Many of us find ourselves on a merry-go-round of well-meaning and misguided 'advice' and recommendations from others. Maybe your boss wants you to develop a skill or competency, perhaps you've had some 'constructive feedback', even worse you may be following the crowd, after all, if everyone else is doing it …

Your boss is just as apt to make misjudgements as you are. Feedback has a stronger foundation in opinion and judgement than fact and the crowd are rushing to Justin Bieber concerts … enough said?

Successful personal development happens when your drive and reason for doing it come from *within* rather than from external pressure. After all, to 'develop' will require personal application, doing things differently, and investing your own time and effort. All of these factors become disproportionately challenging for us when our reasons for development lie with 'others' and external pressures. When your why begins with *I WANT* then you open up a whole new dimension of self-motivation; one that is not easily diverted and rises to life's challenges.

Want is not a dirty word! Turn your *shoulds* into *musts* and then turn your *musts* into *WANTS*.

Who or what inspires you? I'm not talking about a passing interest here, what are you passionate about? What really lights your fire? By honestly answering these questions you'll gain an insight into where your continued development may lie. Choose things that are important and valuable to you, things that excite you and make a real contribution to your world. Those are the things that will get you out of bed in the morning and give you the courage to persevere where others don't.

BITE OFF MORE THAN YOU CAN CHEW!

Your personal development needs to become a habit, something you do instinctively rather than reactively. It should be compelling, exciting, audacious and a little bit scary, something you think about daily. The best way to achieve this is to use as many of your own resources as possible.

We value things we pay for, and those things we pay more for we place greater value in. When we pay with someone else's resources, we are distanced from the investment and therefore value it less. By putting your own resources on the line, you are naturally going to seek to get maximum value for your investment!

Bite off more than you can chew but not so much that you'll choke. Get out of your comfort zone and spend more money on your development than you can reasonably afford. (That doesn't mean sign your life away on the most expensive programme you can find, rather challenge yourself to make the very best 'investment', something you will work hard to provide a return on.)

Commit more of your own time than you have spare. You have the same amount of hours each day as the most successful people on the planet. Over-committing your time will make you examine and re-evaluate your daily routines more critically. Ask yourself, 'If this were my payroll, does this give me best value?' and surprise yourself at how much time you can find. Just 15 minutes a day is the equivalent of 10 hours or more per month!

The first programme I personally paid for was a significant investment of money, time and effort. Something I could little afford at the time. The result? I was fully present for every minute of the four-day seminar. I worked late into the early hours reading and re-reading the material and created habits from what I learned. Do I still remember the seminar? Yes. Do I use the learning? Absolutely and on a daily basis! Have I created a return on my cash investment? Yes … within my very next contract I won using the learning!

MAKE IT SOCIAL, MAKE IT FUN

Your development has a half-life. It's impossible to remember and deploy everything you learn. There's a lot of truth in the saying, 'If you don't use it you lose it' so the sooner you do something (anything!) with your learning, the more chance you have of hanging on to it.

Learning *with* others, especially friends and colleagues, as well as being more fun than solo learning, places a higher level of accountability for action with you; after all, you're more likely to deliver on commitments you make publicly. You can kid yourself you'll take action but your mates will hold you to it!

Support networks multiply your chances of success. Simply sharing your learnings, achievements and difficulties in a safe environment, with people who care about you or who are sharing the journey with you is one of the best learning activities around…and a huge confidence booster. Buddies are a fantastic source of encouragement, challenge and positive recognition, all vital ingredients to your retention and continuing development.

Learning *with* others is fun; learning *for* others takes your development to a whole other level. Neuroscience is showing us in real-time how our brains encode learning for others at a deeper, more emotional level.

When we learn with the goal of teaching others, retention and understanding is higher than with 'selfish' learning.

Set yourself the challenge to present your learning to someone else, or better still 'teach' it on.

Putting it all together

Your confidence is a direct product of your thinking. If that thinking is a constant reminder of your 'failures' and inadequacies in comparison to others, it should be no surprise that your confidence will suffer. If on the other hand that thinking is a constant reminder of your growth and development and improvement … then what will be the impact on your confidence?

Growth and development – knowing you are better today than you were last year has long been advocated as a 'need' for all of us. When we stop learning, we stop growing and start dying.

Scientists and researchers are now proposing continuous learning as a defence against age-related illnesses such as Alzheimer's and dementia.

Much of this is yet to be proved by science so for me, if for no other reason than 'being alive', *active, regular* and *meaningful* personal development must be on every confident person's to-do list.

[With thanks for the material in this chapter to Steve Marriott – www.steve-marriott.com]

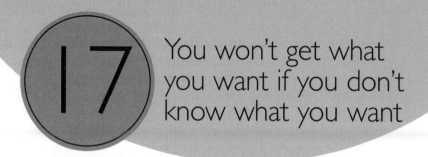

17 You won't get what you want if you don't know what you want

> **❝** *There are always flowers for those who want to see them.*
> Henri Matisse

> **❝** *It isn't sufficient just to want – you've got to ask yourself what you are going to do to get the things you want.*
> Franklin D. Roosevelt

> **❝** *You can't cross the sea merely by standing and staring at the water.* Rabindranath Tagore

> **❝** *Don't be afraid to take a big step if one is indicated. You can't cross a chasm in two small jumps.* David Lloyd George

> **❝** *A man's reach should exceed his grasp, or what's heaven for?*
> Robert Browning

Whether you are in business or sport, education or parenting, the practice of setting goals for yourself or others is a familiar one. My experience is that people with a genuine and consistent sense of confidence goal-set regularly and naturally, and in a way that works best for them. The art and science of finding what works for you is certainly one of the secrets of confident people.

First let us look at why goal-setting works in the first place. Your brain is fundamentally wired to follow commands that it is given. You will see the importance of this predisposition for the brain to obey commands (up to a point) in various other chapters of this book and it is the core factor in understanding the power of goal-setting. Various research suggests that we are exposed to somewhere between 20 million and 400 billion bits of data every second. Our brain can process around 1000 every second and we are consciously aware of around 20 things every second. This deleting and filtering of information and awareness helps us to function. Without it we would effectively be in constant data overwhelm. What we focus on changes what data is filtered in and out of our awareness. I would like you to notice for a moment the temperature of your left little toe. Whatever the temperature is my guess is that you had forgotten you had a left little toe before I brought it back into your awareness. This is a simple example of this brain activity in action.

By setting confidence-related goals you will direct your brain to filter in more information that is relevant to the achievement of those goals. You will also become more aware of resources, skills and abilities that you already have at your disposal.

MAKE THE GOAL COMPELLING FOR YOU

Let me be really clear that I don't believe there is one best way to set goals. There are many systems that profess to be the best. Theories are presented and debunked in equal measure. The nature of human beings means that there will never be a one size fits all for goal-setting, but a choice of good practices that you can combine to be the best process for you.

The single most important question seems to be what will make this goal compelling for you? In some cases it will be the topic of the goal that makes it exciting for you. In others it will be the specificity of it. Some people will prefer making the goal really achievable so that progress can be reviewed, while for others the fun of the pursuit of an outrageous idealistic goal is completely energizing.

Let us explore a simple confidence-related aim to understand what makes goals compelling for you: the goal of walking into a room confidently and feeling confident.

What would have to happen to make that a compelling goal for you? Would it be the specificity of which room with which people under which circumstances? For example, walking into a boardroom full of executives to present a proposal with your heart rate and breathing remaining at a normal level.

If achievable goals energize you, you will be more motivated by setting a number of progressive goals:

> **Week 1:** Walk into a room full of strangers while remaining calm.
> **Week 2:** Walk into a room for a one-to-one conversation with a senior manager while remaining calm.
> **Week 3:** Ask a question in a meeting with executives while remaining calm.
> **Week 4:** Walk in to the room while remaining completely calm.

If you are energized by the process of working towards audacious and unrealistic goals then you might set a goal like 'stride confidently into a board meeting while completely naked and greet each person individually'. I am sure I don't need to say that the aim is not to actually do this, but the game in finding the strategies that would enable you to achieve the goal will make it easy to do something more realistic and sensible.

Choose a confidence goal that is relevant to you and write it in different ways with emphasis on different elements until you find the version that feels most compelling for you.

USE YOUR GOALS AND SHARE THEM APPROPRIATELY

In Chapter 15 we explored the power of creating pictorial representations of your future history. This can be hugely powerful for general goal-setting too. A former boss of mine had a huge collage of all of his goals for the next 12 months set out in a time line. He kept it in a prominent place in his office and was happy to share it with anyone who was interested. This sharing kept him engaged and on track and the visual element made it compelling for him.

My goals tend to be written and in my early days as a leadership consultant my confidence-related goals were a simple list of milestones. I referred to them infrequently but reviewed them monthly. This prevented me from becoming overly obsessed with them but ensured I made regular progress.

This should emphasize again that there is not one ideal format for presenting goals or for how often they should be reviewed. There will be a preferred process for you and I would encourage you to try different approaches to find the one that energizes you most.

The same applies to whether you should share your confidence goals with others. Throughout my formative years in the fields of personal development the mantra was to share your goals. The belief was that the more people you shared them with the more likely you were to follow through with the actions required to achieve that goal. In more recent times the belief has switched with social psychologists citing experiments showing that the process of sharing tricks the brain into believing you have already taken action or, worse, that scorn from others will demotivate you from following through, showing that the process of sharing goals can trick the brain into believing you have already achieved them. Having those that you share them with ridicule the goals will also demotivate and disengage.

Both of these views are relevant and over-simplistic. For example, if someone tells you that you won't achieve something, does this make you more likely to go out and prove them wrong or does it de-energize you? Do all people have the same impact on you? For each goal that you set think carefully about who would be most useful to share it with. You don't have to share any with anyone, but I usually find that there is someone in my social or business network who is likely to hold me accountable to action or motivate me to do so.

Goals should motivate and engage you into action; being mindful of how you use them and who you share them with will add fuel to them.

TRY MAKING FAILURE-BASED GOALS

The most consistent theme in studies that question the power of goals is the stress that goals or their non-achievement can cause. In my view this isn't a challenge with goal-setting, but in the goals themselves. Goals should energize and engage. They should trigger a desire to do something. If your goals do anything other than this, go back to the beginning of this chapter and revise them with the ideas and advice in mind.

It is also useful to know that some people are motivated by the desire to achieve goals and others are motivated by the desire not to fail. This doesn't change the impact of goals, but will influence how you write or create them. Think for a moment about what gives you the energy to take action. Is it the desire to move towards, having things or achieving, or is it about moving away from where you are now and not settling for what you have? If you are motivated by moving away from where you are now, then be sure to integrate that language into your goals.

Putting it all together

Well-executed goal-setting is a powerful tool in any part of life. If you are in pursuit of a strong sense of confidence, then you can only know when you have achieved what you set out to do by having goals in place that clearly define what confidence looks, sounds and feels like for you.

There is no single best formula for the creation and review of goals. You have to use the best of what we know works for some, to create the recipe that fits you perfectly. Goal-setting is a regular practice for the confident. In some cases they don't realize they do it. They consistently set and adjust their goals and take their achievement as a sign of progress. Others consciously set goals and use them as fuel for growth and success.

Goals should create energy and the most confident people understand that. They also understand that none-achievement of the goal does not mean failure. You define your goals, your goals do not define you.

18 Focus on what you can change

❝ *There are three constants in life … Change, choice and principles.*
Stephen Covey

❝ *You can't depend on your eyes when your imagination is out of focus.* Mark Twain

❝ *I find hope in the darkest of days, and focus in the brightest. I do not judge the universe.* Dalai Lama

❝ *I don't focus on what I'm up against. I focus on my goals and I try to ignore the rest.* Venus Williams

❝ *My life didn't please me, so I created my life.* Coco Chanel

Many of you will be familiar with the opening few lines of the serenity prayer:

God grant me the serenity to
accept the things I cannot change;
courage to change the things I can;
and wisdom to know the difference.

(From the 'Serenity Prayer' by Reinhold Niebuhr)

These few lines encapsulate beautifully one of the characteristics of highly confident people. They have developed the ability to focus on changing the areas of their life that they can exercise some control over, not worrying about the areas that they can't.

The perception of a lack of choice is one of the biggest inhibitors of confidence. It can be mentally paralysing and this is why I love the principle that 'any choice is better than no choice'.

Dr Stephen Covey presented a quite wonderful framework to develop this way of thinking in his seminal book *The 7 Habits of Highly Effective People*.

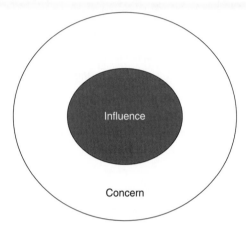

The influence circle represents all of the things that you can make a difference to in any situation or area of your life. The concern circle represents everything that causes concern that you can't do anything about. It is useful to remember that this is a model of attention as well as action.

In any area of your life the circle that you focus on will grow and the other will conversely shrink. I think this is due to both psychological and practical reasons. Research suggests we can consciously pay attention to somewhere around 20 things at a time. If we fill our conscious attention with things that would fall into the circle of concern then we have less thinking space left to notice anything we can change. This leaves us with a genuine sense that we can't change anything. Of course this is very rarely the case but it feels very real and drains confidence and certainty.

Fortunately the opposite is also true. If you consciously focus on all of the things that you can change in any situation, then the space in your thinking for the aspects that worry you but that you can't change reduces. Psychologically your circle of influence grows and your circle of concern reduces.

In addition there are practical implications. Consider for a moment you are influenced by someone who is energetic, has a 'can do' attitude and always seems to get things moving. Now contrast this with someone who is negative, constantly focuses on what is wrong and has little idea of what to do next; how likely are they to get what they want from you? It seems obvious to me that those who focus on their circle of influence are by nature going to be able to influence those around them more and have a great support network. In turn, due to their connections, they are going to have increasing ability to get things done. This further feeds their circle of influence and so on. The opposite is also true. Those who focus their attention and (ever decreasing) energy on what can't be changed are less likely to be able to influence people around them and therefore find it even more difficult to get what they want. This proves their thinking, expands their circle of concern and reduces their influence further and the cycle carries on.

A focus on what you can change fuels confidence and an increased state of confidence will fuel the sense that you can influence the world around you. This is a healthy cycle to be in. Before you continue, take a moment to reflect on where you naturally focus. If your tendency is to worry about what you can't change then this will inhibit your confidence. Use this chapter to begin to change your focus.

BE INFLUENTIAL AT WORK

Over the past ten years I have been lucky enough to work with some fantastic organizations, from global sector leaders through to companies voted as some of the top employers in the UK. Even within these organizations it is common for people to carry a sense that they can't make a difference beyond the straightforward task that they have been employed to do. Innovation is more often restricted by an individual's thinking than by a dismissive boss. More opportunities to grow relationships are missed because an individual thinks that they can't improve a connection and therefore doesn't try, than by actual disagreements in the work place.

If you are facing any significant challenges at work, then take the time now to review what you can change and separate it from what you can't. Even if the elements that you would place in the circle of influence seem small it is important to focus on them and that action.

During my development programmes I am often asked for strategies on influencing upwards. I have begun to remind participants about the serenity prayer and the circles of influence and concern. The question isn't, 'How can I influence my boss?', but, 'What can I influence my boss on?' No one is 100 per cent set on every opinion and worldview, so consider where you are able to make a difference and focus on that.

The same applies to project work. If you find yourself with a sense that a project is going off-track and there is nothing you can do about it, then take time to use the circles of influence and concern to explore where to place your energy and focus.

FOCUS ON WHAT YOU CAN DO IN RELATIONSHIPS

A coach of mine once suggested that we create our partners and relationships. He shared that whenever he had negative thoughts about things his wife did, she seemed to magically do more of those things. He experimented with writing a list of all the things that he loved about her and placed special attention on the characteristics that most endeared her to him. He never shared the list with her but would still begin to notice more and more of these wonderful traits.

There is a lesson in this when it comes to our focus in relationships. I see so many people in relationships focusing on the things in their partner that make them unhappy. I would suggest that this is unhealthy and can only lead to a suffocation of any love and connection.

I don't believe that any healthy relationship is built on a foundation of control and few survive when one partner has a drive to change the other. If you want a great relationship a great question to ask is, 'What can I influence?' The primary answer to this is you. You can influence the decisions you make, your health, how you dress, what you choose to make important and even whether to stay with someone.

These things may in turn influence others' choices and behaviours but this has to be seen as a potential outcome not a sole purpose.

I am an expert on confidence not relationships. I am lucky enough to have a wonderful wife and I've made many mistakes along the way. One thing I am certain of is that truly confident people know when to give everything they can to a relationship and when to say enough is enough.

FOCUS ON YOUR CHOICES

Have you ever had a moment when you felt that you had no choice in life? The sense that you can't influence anything is one of the quickest ways to emotionally overwhelm and will wipe out confidence. It is no surprise then that I work hard to ensure clients understand that they always have a choice. You have an ultimate choice right now. You could decide to never move again. This might not be a compelling choice, but it is a choice none the less. Eventually someone would come along and move you somehow. They may even take you somewhere warm and padded, hose you down and force you to have some food. I would like to think that the realization that you have that option will make whatever else you are doing now more compelling. As I said earlier in the chapter, any choice is better than no choice. Even in the darkest moments you have options. You decide whether to eat healthily or not. You choose to make family time more important than exercise. You choose who you spend time with and how much importance you place on the opinions of others.

There are times when it doesn't feel like you have a choice. You will often feel that you have to go to work. Even in this there is a choice. You could not go. The implications would probably be even less desirable than going, but it is still a choice.

At any moment when you feel there is no choice in life, go back to good old Dr Covey's model and work out what is in your circle of influence. Its simple power can change everything.

Putting it all together

Confident people create a cycle of influence where they are thinking about what they can do. This means they do more, which means they think they can do more and so the cycle continues. Focusing on what you can influence has the wonderful side-effect of filtering out thoughts of what you can't do anything about.

The ultimate choice that we have is what thoughts to pay most attention to. Confident people take the 'you can't do it' mind-talk with a huge pinch of salt and pay more attention to the 'let's see if we can' internal conversations. The final step is to take action . Have the courage to change the things that you can.

19 Focus on solutions

❝ *There are some four million different kinds of animals and plants in the world. Four million different solutions to the problems of staying alive.* David Attenborough

❝ *I think that all comics or humorists, or whatever we are, ask questions.*
That's what we're supposed to do.
But I not only ask the questions, I offer solutions. Roseanne Barr

❝ *Never bring the problem-solving stage into the decision-making stage. Otherwise, you surrender yourself to the problem rather than the solution.* Robert H. Schuller

❝ *There are no problems. Only Solutions.* John Lennon

❝ *Most people spend more time and energy going around problems than in trying to solve them.* Henry Ford

In life it is certain that problems will occur. We all have challenges to overcome and our process for examining and overcoming these problems will have significant impact on our confidence. I noticed some years ago that the most confident people in my network seemed to focus on working out solutions rather than explaining and analysing problems.

While I think there is a place for exploring problems and analysing them to prevent them happening again, I believe there is too much emphasis placed on this in most coaching, counselling and therapies. In previous chapters I have shared the concept that we can consciously pay attention to around 20 things at once. An over-emphasis on exploring life's challenges can easily lead to our awareness being completely filled by a single problem.

The antidote of this immersion in problems is solutions-focused thinking. This approach has its roots in the therapeutic approach devised by Steve de Shazer and Insoo Kim Berg and others, at the Brief Family Therapy Centre, Milwaukee. This approach values simplicity in philosophy and language and aims to discover what works in a given situation simply and practically.

One of the key elements is the absence of any focus on the problem. The attention instead is on where you are now, where you want to be and the discovery of small steps to get there.

My own experience of solutions-focused thinking is that it has positively impacted on every area of my life. For anyone whose work includes coaching, working with teams or managing change I would highly recommend *The Solutions Focus* by Mark McKergow and Paul Z. Jackson.

One of the great benefits of solutions-focused thinking is the immediacy of results. It will help you to see that you are closer to a solution than you first thought and that you can move even closer quickly and easily. This is always going to build confidence and encourage you to do more.

A SOLUTIONS-BASED GOAL

I once observed a coaching session where the coach asked the coachee, 'How do you know this is a big problem?' The reply lasted some time during which the coaching became increasingly immersed in the situation and linked together several previously unrelated problems. With one question the coach expanded the size of the problem in the coachee's mind. I stepped in at this point and asked a similarly simple question that changed the focus of the coachee's thinking completely:

'Imagine you went to bed tonight and while you were asleep a miracle happened and that problem completely disappeared.

When you woke up how would you know that the miracle had happened?'

Ask yourself this question about a challenge that you have in your life right now. Answer the question in as much rich detail as you possibly can. You will notice two things. Firstly you will get really clear on where you want to get to. This is another way of creating a clear and compelling goal. Secondly you will notice a very different state compared to the state that would be generated if I asked you to explore the nature of the problem you were faced with. When you combine these two aspects, the effect is only ever going to be positive.

IDENTIFY WHERE THE SOLUTION IS HAPPENING ALREADY

Having defined the outcome it is useful to explore whether there are situations where the solution already happens. Think back to the challenge you have just been considering and answer this question: on a scale of one to ten, where ten is the ideal future you have just defined, where are you now?

In answering this question many people notice that they are closer to their desired end point than they first realized. I have coached clients specifically about confidence using this approach and having initially described how they had no confidence and it was inhibiting them in every part of their life they then scaled themselves as a five against their miracle future. When I reflect back to them that they are half way towards a future they have defined as ideal there is a palpable shift in thinking.

Now consider what has got you that high up the scale. No matter what score you initially gave yourself – even if your response was a one, reflect on what makes it a one rather than a zero. For many people analysing why a score is low rather than why it is high is counter-intuitive, however this exploration of what is already working is a key step in sorting for the positive. If we can understand what is working for us already in any challenging situation – no matter how small this may be – and do more of it, we are already on the way to tackling the issue.

TAKE SMALL STEPS TO PROGRESS

Step back for a moment to the scaling that you did against your miracle future. As you reflect on where you are now, ask yourself what would have to happen to move you just one small step up the scale. For example if you were a four out of ten what would have to happen to take you to a five?

This is a super-simple but vital step in focusing on the positive. One of the challenges with setting big goals is that they can seem so difficult to achieve. By defining the smallest steps, and then acting on them, you will see and feel the signs of progress. Moving towards the end-goal always feeds confidence and encourages action. You may find though that the simple steps which you identify as those that will take you from a three to a four will actually move you from a three to a seven or eight. There is beauty in simplicity and there is energy in action.

Putting it all together

Over the past ten years there has been a huge wave of research in the fields of positive thinking and psychology. While some of this research requires more validation, it is clear that sorting for the positive does more than simply make you feel better. Those who are able to take a solutions-focused approach to life's challenges are likely to be more productive, more influential and get better results. The latest wave of evidence seems to suggest that positive thinking even has health benefits and my experience is certainly that those who focus mainly on the problems in their life seem to become ill more often.

One additional tip for anchoring this mindset is to reflect, review and analyse when things have gone unexpectedly brilliantly. All too often I see organizations and individuals carrying out large-scale reviews that have somehow gone wrong. This chapter has described the limitations of this already, but these limitations are turned on their heads with an in-depth analysis of what went right – especially when it wasn't predicted.

The link to confidence is a direct one. In sorting for the positive you are confirming what you can do and reducing the time and energy you have to focus on what you can't. You will retrain your brain to notice more of the positive and resourceful situations and people in your life. By applying the philosophy of the solutions-focused thinking community you will develop a framework for solving the challenges that life inevitably throws up. All of these will further endorse your psyche as someone who is able to flex and adapt in any situation and feel positive while doing it. This is the heart of real long-term confidence.

20 Positivity creates confidence

CC *One love, one heart, one destiny.* Bob Marley

CC *Keep your face always toward the sunshine – and shadows will fall behind you.* Walt Whitman

CC *You can, you should, and if you're brave enough to start, you will.* Stephen King

CC *A pessimist sees the difficulty in every opportunity; an optimist sees the opportunity in every difficulty.* Winston Churchill

CC *A man is but the product of his thoughts what he thinks, he becomes.* Mahatma Gandhi

Pronoia (pronounced pronoya): the suspicion that the universe is a conspiracy on your behalf.

Imagine the effect on your confidence if you believed that the whole universe and everything in it was working in your favour. It might sound like a crazy thought to have, but let me give an example of someone who has the opposite belief and what their working day is like:

The alarm goes off. It is 5:45am and you have resolved to get up early, and have some breakfast before going to the gym. It is Monday and it is January, time for a new start. It is also two below zero and you forgot to reset the heating to take account of your early start. Damn that heating timer.

You decide to go to the gym tomorrow and hit snooze to have an extra 30 minutes in bed before getting up for an early start.

You wake with a start at 7:00am. The useless alarm didn't go off – granted you didn't actually press snooze, just thought about it – and it's a good job that your delightful children have got their lazy backsides out of bed. Just how did you get chosen to parent the loudest kids in living history?

You jump out of bed, stub your toe – who put that chair there? – and jump into a now luke-warm shower as the kids have used all the hot water. You wrap yourself in a damp towel and head downstairs to fumble about for the iron. Why the hell wasn't there enough time at the weekend to get a couple of shirts ironed?

You are now dressed in your roughly ironed cloths and your stress levels are heading towards the top of the scale. Of course the car is freezing and the traffic is a nightmare – it looks like every Tom, Dick and Harriet is late this morning too. Either that or they are just getting in your way specifically to irritate you. Then there are the roadworks – especially designed by the gas emergency people to make you even more unpopular with your boss and clients.

You finally arrive at the office 35 minutes late, which of course means there is more chance of being given a 100 per cent pay rise today than getting a parking space in the staff car park. Having trudged to work in the rain from the ridiculously remote overflow car park, which was strategically placed in another postcode by the planners and architects, you finally arrive to find there is already the biggest pile of files, customer complaints and requests from everyone from the Chief Executive to your most troublesome team member.

Oh and the email is down.

And the phones.

And your mobile is just about to go flat as you forgot to charge it last night.

Why does technology do that to you? It's almost as if the universe is working against you just to make life as difficult as possible and the working day has not even begun yet!

I can feel my energy levels have dropped even writing this example; it is no wonder that those of you who suffer this kind of experience every day feel so tired in the morning that you think you need a cocktail of coffee, energy drinks and sugar to get you through the day.

If you want to experience confidence more of the time, then one great option is to start showing signs of *pronoia*.

Pronoia is the unwavering belief that the whole universe and everybody and everything is conspiring to help you in every way that is possible.

Most people have an immediate response that this is plain stupid. But if you have lived even part of the example above, then you are happy to make the assumption that the universe and things within it are conspiring against you. You are also living in a world where people who you have never met are doing things to get in your way. The beliefs that you are living your life by are just as improbable as *pronoia*.

BE PRONOID

Pronoid travel includes believing that there is a special policeman travelling half a mile ahead of your car ensuring that the traffic is flowing smoothly for you. The only time he will allow you to be slowed down is when it is for your own safety. The universe will also ensure that you catch exactly the aeroplane, train or boat that you are supposed to. This will usually be the one you book, but if there is some reason for an alternative, it will do that. Trust it is the best for you.

Pronoid relationships mean that you will be with the person you are supposed to be with for exactly as long as you are supposed to be with them in order for you both to learn all of the lessons that you are meant to. You will not meet before the time is due, nor will you be allowed to stay together beyond what is right.

If a relationship ends, it is for entirely good reasons, even if you cannot see that yet.

Pronoid careers work in a similar way. If you have defined what you want from your career and/or your life, the universe is making it happen right now. That means every redundancy is planned, every challenging boss you have is there for a reason, and restructures strengthen your position in the long term, if not the short term.

PLAN FOR THE BEST

Many of my coaching clients start our relationship with a belief that they should assume, and therefore plan for, the worst. This includes how they travel, how they plan their finances, relationships and more.

I am not advocating a *laissez-faire* approach to life, nor a high-risk one; I think planning is a good thing, but over-doing it leads to problems too. The brain is pretty much wired to give us more of what we focus on, so consistently planning for the worst dramatically increases the likelihood of us getting exactly that.

Thinking about relationships in a pronoid way might involve deciding what you are looking for in a relationship and putting yourself in situations where you might meet people who are looking for similar. The opposite would mean that you get really desperate and go with the next person who shows any interest in you and then blame the world for your unhappiness.

Planning a trip in a pronoid way would include checking the weather and packing based on that. If something unexpected comes along you can always buy or borrow something. Paranoid planning would mean packing for every single possible eventuality, incurring baggage charges at the airport or an aching back from carrying cases. It would also end in wondering why there is so much washing and ironing to do when you get home.

This should be straightforward, but I meet people every day who believe the world is against them and blame the results of bad decision making on that.

NOTICE RESULTS OF PRONOIA

If you have been reading this book diligently you will understand that sorting for the positive will help you to feel better, more confident and you are likely to notice different things about yourself and the world around you. What may still surprise you is that developing a positive mind set will increase your chances of success in life. Shawn Achor shares some enlightening research in his book, *The Happiness Advantage,* that demonstrates the power of sorting for the positive. For example, college freshmen who were empirically shown to be happy had a higher income 19 years earlier than their unhappy classmates. His research also suggests that happy people are 31 per cent more productive than those who are negative, neutral or stressed. An increasing amount of solid research points to the fact that pronoia, or at least training yourself to sort for the positive, will help you to make better decisions more quickly, to be more productive and potentially even earn more money.

Reflect on the results of your pronoia. Use them as fuel to build an even more pronoid approach.

Putting it all together

Most of us are brought up in a model of the world that suggests that when we have a certain amount of money or achieve a certain level of success then we will be happy. I am more certain than ever this flawed world view is a key contributory factor to a lack of confidence. Shawn Achor is among a growing band of researchers who are demonstrating that training ourselves to be positive and happy leads to success and high performance. Adopting a pronoic view of the universe is a great way to start this process. Clients who have experimented with this almost irrationally positive view of life consistently report that they are experiencing better luck than before and the ability to do more or achieve things than previously. Success and confidence shouldn't be linked but if they were, sorting for the positive is a great way to kick-start both.

21 Luck and confidence

I'm a greater believer in luck, and I find the harder I work the more I have of it. Thomas Jefferson

The more I practice, the luckier I get. Gary Player

Shallow men believe in luck or in circumstance. Strong men believe in cause and effect. Ralph Waldo Emerson

Ability is of little account without opportunity. Lucille Ball

Luck is believing you're lucky. Tennessee Williams

There appears to be some connection between luck and confidence. Lucky people seem to meet their perfect partners and achieve lifelong ambitions. They have great careers and seem to win regularly at games of chance. Highly confident people seem to experience the same luck and from the outside their luck will boost their confidence. This is a perfectly rational assumption to make, but a study of the characteristics and behaviours of lucky people and a similar understanding of the highly confident shows a significant correlation. So the good news is that by reading and applying the techniques in this book you get to be more confident AND experience more luck!

It is useful at this stage to distinguish between fortune and luck. Fortune is an unknown and unpredictable phenomenon. Luck is what we experience and is predictable and influenceable. A decade ago I read a book that opened my eyes to just how subjective our luck is. I would highly recommend *The Luck Factor* by Dr Richard Wiseman. Dr Wiseman presents a simple and easy-to-follow explanation as to why some people are lucky and others unlucky. Through a set of well constructed studies and experiments he also provides a framework for anyone to experience more luck in their lives. I am in no doubt that applying the techniques in his book will lead to a greater sense of luck as well as confidence and applying his experiments will result in a greater confidence.

The number one step is to decide whether you can be lucky. Due to the nature of human experience the moment that you decide you are a lucky person, or at least experience luck, then your experience of it changes. Conversely it is extremely difficult to be lucky if you don't think you are a lucky person. And even if you are you won't notice it! It is no coincidence at all that many highly confident people also consider themselves to be at least moderately lucky.

NOTICE WHEN YOU ARE LUCKY

I am always shocked when I see people on television declaring that they have never won anything in their lives. These are often people who have already won the opportunity to be on a game show or reality TV show ahead of thousands of other people. I find it hard to believe that people can reach advanced adulthood never having won *anything*. If you are able to stop reading for a moment and list anything and everything that you have ever won, this could be from games of chance (ever won a goldfish at the funfair or a toy at an amusement arcade?) to something you have to work harder for (an award at school, swimming certificate or an accolade at work?). I surveyed a small group of people when writing this chapter. Sixty per cent responded to the question, 'Tell me something you have won' with an immediate response that they hadn't won anything before. When probed further only two per cent actually couldn't recall winning anything.

Not all of these instances will have been down to luck, but this does reinforce the idea that lucky people notice when luck happens. Unlucky people seem to delete lucky occurrences in their life.

What do you define as luck in your life? Does the moment that you met your partner count as good luck? Are you lucky to have great kids or the job that you enjoy? Do you think that the fact that you have great friends makes you lucky?

The more luck you define yourself as having, the luckier a person you are. The luckier a person you define yourself as, the more luck you will experience.

LOOK FOR THE LUCK IN YOUR BAD LUCK

One of the favourite elements of Dr Wiseman's research on luck is that lucky people see the positive in their bad luck. I see this principle played out in many people that I work with. In organizations or teams which are going through periods of change this is a major factor in defining the culture while change is taking place.

Imagine this scenario. The company you work for decides to restructure. As a result of it you retain your job at the same level and salary. Your boss, who you regard highly, leaves the organization and you now report to a former colleague who you believe is less skilled than you. Do you consider this lucky or unlucky?

What about this situation? You lose your purse or wallet. In it is some cash and your credit cards. You also have some small items of sentimental value. Having cancelled all of your credit cards you find them along with the cash and personal items in a place you hadn't checked in your house. Again do you consider this lucky or unlucky?

If you want to feel luckier in situations such as these, focus on the positive comparison to what could have been rather than the negative. In these situations that would be a realization that you could have been the one made redundant and be looking for a job just before Christmas. It's better to have a job even with a boss that you aren't sure of than to have no job at all. In situation two at least you have your cash and personal items back; most people who lose a wallet or purse never see any of it again.

Focusing on the negative comparison will help you train your brain to look for the negatives in situations and to forget experiences of good luck. This in turn can make it harder to trigger your confidence.

BUILD YOUR LUCK NETWORK

In the same way that having a network of confident people will reinforce your sense of confidence, spending time with lucky people will enhance your sense of luck.

Imagine surrounding yourself with people whose main hope in life is to solve their financial worries by playing bingo, gambling on horses and playing the lottery. Guess how lucky these people see themselves and their lives? And as you saw more data from these people that bad luck was the only luck available to them this would influence your sense of luck. I chose this example very specifically because it reflects the experience of many of the older generation I grew up with. Don't fall into that trap.

Take and make every opportunity that you can to surround yourself with people who seem to be lucky. Interact with them and learn from their luck. If they can make their own luck, then understand how they do it and apply the principles in your life. I have two friends who the rest of my social circle consider to be the luckiest people we know. It is no surprise to me that when they attend social events at the local racecourse they join together and form a betting alliance. Whether it is good planning or good fortune, these two luck conductors always finish 'up' on their flutters. While some of my friends scorn their lucky breaks, one or two smart ones spend their time looking over their shoulders and following their wagers.

Who are the luckiest people that you know career wise, in relationships or in health? How can you connect with them even more closely and make them part of your luck network?

Putting it all together

Throughout this book I have reinforced the key point that your confidence is within your control. Many people who haven't read this book will think that confidence is something which happens as a result of external factors. The same applies to luck. While nature or fortune defines where we are born and our presence at certain events we can have a huge influence on the luck that we experience.

This is both from the perspective of the amount of luck that we actually need or notice and the opportunities for good luck to happen to us. If you turn your luck radar up you will experience an increasing amount of luck. By seeing more positives in your bad luck, you refocus your brain even more on the positive, and by absorbing what others who are lucky do, you are creating more opportunities to feel the luck that they do.

The cumulative effect of this on your confidence is unquestionable. Confidence and luck form a powerful partnership. One feeds the other and, alongside the foundation techniques from the early part of this book, you will be able to have a tremendously positive influence on others around you who feel that they are lacking in either of these.

I'll leave the final words of the chapter to Dr Wiseman: 'When it comes to luck, the future is in your hands.'

And it starts right now.

22 Confidence before success

> **❝** I believe in intuitions and inspirations ... I sometimes FEEL that I am right. I do not KNOW that I am. Albert Einstein

> **❝** There is no such uncertainty as a sure thing. Robert Burns

> **❝** Modest doubt is called the beacon of the wise. William Shakespeare

> **❝** Live life as though nobody is watching, and express yourself as though everyone is listening. Nelson Mandela

> **❝** I think self-awareness is probably the most important thing towards being a champion. Billie Jean King

There is a fundamental flaw in the way that many of us think about confidence. These flaws have brought me many coaching clients over the years and caused stress to millions of people in business, sport and in personal lives.

Take the example of the million-pound footballer. I worked with a player who had already had a successful career in the second and third tiers of English football. When he secured a £1 million-plus deal to sign for a Premier League club you would expect that his confidence would shoot through the roof. After all, in a footballer's career that is classed as success and of course his long-term financial security was assured. Instead, the primary emotion he experienced throughout his first year in the top flight was insecurity.

I have seen this pattern repeated within organizations when individuals secure long worked-for promotions. Also in relationships when an individual finds their life partner and instead of confidence they experience tremendous concern about losing that partner.

Each of these examples shows that achievement doesn't necessarily lead to confidence. More often, an achievement of what we have labelled as an indicator of success will impact our ability to feel confidence. Continued success in the new role or relationship will help to reinstate that challenged confidence but this chapter, along with the rest of the book, will reinforce that the formula should be reversed. Results in every area of your life will be delivered and maintained through establishing your deep genuine confidence first. Don't get caught in the confidence trap.

BUILD CONFIDENCE TO GET WHAT YOU WANT NOT THE OTHER WAY AROUND

It is important to remember that confidence leads to success and achievement and not necessarily the other way around. Let's turn this into a very simple formula for the purpose of this section.

In this case C represents the confidence that you are building. It must be a genuine confidence rather than surface arrogance, and it must be a confidence that continues to be embedded as part of who you are. In some instances you may look to build your confidence in specific areas such as those represented in this book. In other instances you will build your confidence with a specific end goal or situation in mind.

The A in the equation represents the other things that you can do to support your success. For example, if you are preparing for a job interview then ensure that your confidence (C) is high but take action (A) to ensure that you have researched the company and role well. If your success relates to performance in a specific job then keep building and developing your confidence (C) but also take consistent action (A) on your personal development to ensure you have the skills and abilities to continue to develop the role.

Consider this simple equation for every key area of your life. Support your confidence-building with simple and consistent actions that speed up or maintain your success.

DEVELOP CONFIDENCE TO MATCH YOUR GOALS

As I have described elsewhere, goal-setting is a useful aid to confidence. To feel a sense of achievement or success you need to define what that success looks like. Consistent action is also valuable. One of the common traits of confident and successful people who I meet is that they take action rather than procrastinating. However avoiding the confidence trap requires you to let go of the assumption that being successful and action-orientated results in confidence. People who are successful without anchoring their confidence usually become stressed due to their consistent and nagging self-doubt. I often hear people in this situation talking about the sense that one day they will be found out. If you find yourself with this feeling then it is a sure-fire cue for you to bolster your confidence.

Those who are successful and take lots of action without the foundation of confidence become tired and stressed and still don't have that fundamental belief in themselves that underpins them. This is a sure-fire route to burnout.

As your goals get evermore challenging then you may need to further develop your confidence. Make this an integral part of your strategy for achieving what you want. As your success becomes even more apparent be sure to bring your confidence with you. It can be at moments of great achievement that your confidence wobbles most. Do not expect your confidence to always grow with your success. In the moments that it does then that is wonderful but don't let the moments when this doesn't happen take you by surprise.

FEEL THE FEAR AND …

The late Susan Jeffers wrote the fabulously titled self-help classic *Feel The Fear and Do It Anyway*. This title should stay with you as you continue to avoid the confidence trap. When you aren't sure what to do, do something. When fear holds you back or thoughts of 'I will when …' take hold, then move. The chapter on fear in this book (Chapter 2) will help you to understand why you are feeling the way you are and the chapter on taking action (Chapter 29) will help you to do something about it, but the sooner you do something positive the more likely you will be to notice your confidence growing and the more you will achieve what you want to achieve more quickly too.

> Don't take the unhelpful mind-chatter of 'I might not be ready for this' as advice not to do it. Give yourself the opportunity to experiment with success, and while achievement doesn't guarantee you confidence, action-orientation does give fuel for more of both. What is the very next step that you could take right now that would change your perception of how successful you can be? What could you do in the next 24 hours that might be a little uncomfortable but would help get momentum? Got the answer? Then go and do it!

Putting it all together

I would love every person who reads this book to be more successful. That includes you. I would like you to be wealthier and to have more of the cool things in life that you really want. Few things would help me to be happier than to hear that you have the job, house and relationship that you want. I also want to be clear that these things are not guaranteed to give you confidence. Being in a relationship with a gorgeous man or beautiful woman is as likely to reduce your confidence as it is to increase it. A fantastic new job or the creation of your own business will give you less certainty rather than more. Even having more money can lead to more fear, not less. I am not trying to put you off success and wealth but to encourage you to prepare for it. Get confident first. Make it strong, genuine and a state that you lapse into without realizing. Take action that affects the outside world as your confidence builds and notice results.

Confidence and action will lead to achievement. Be sure to nurture your confidence as your life becomes richer (in every sense of the word) and you will continue to be fulfilled. Avoid the confidence trap at all costs and the world will remain your oyster.

23 The physiology of confidence

❝ *What you do speaks so loud that I cannot hear what you say.*
Ralph Waldo Emerson

❝ *Body language is a very powerful tool. We had body language before we had speech, and apparently, 80 per cent of what you understand in a conversation is read through the body, not the words.* Deborah Bull

❝ *The most important thing in communication is hearing what isn't said.* Peter F. Drucker

❝ *Language is a more recent technology. Your body language, your eyes, your energy will come through to your audience before you even start speaking.* Peter Guber

❝ *I see tendencies, I see body language.* Michael Chang

In November of 2012 I watched a brilliant TED Talk that would forever change my view on the power that our body has on our confidence. I want to thank Dr Amy Cuddy for her fantastic work in the field of social psychology and acknowledge the impact that has had on my work and on my clients.

Imagine being able to change how other people perceive not only your levels of confidence but also competency in just two minutes. Dr Cuddy and her colleagues at the Hellman Faculty at Harvard University found that by adopting certain poses for just two minutes significantly affected not just how individuals felt, but how others perceived them. In one of the team's most powerful experiments, individuals were brought into a laboratory and asked to adopt high or low-power poses (more on what these are later in the chapter). They then took part in a thorough and very stressful job interview. As well as being observed and videoed the interviewer was trained to give zero non-verbal feedback. When the videos of these hugely demanding interviews were sent to independent reviewers they selected all the people who had adopted high-power poses and rejected all those who had adopted low-power poses. The adoption of these simple poses allows you to be at your confident best so quickly that it can impact not just how you feel but how others perceive your capability.

I have invited hundreds of people to experiment with power poses since I began following Dr Cuddy's work, and the impact has been remarkable. Clients have shared stories of significantly better performance at work and in job interviews, being able to give keynote speeches when previously the thought of presenting to even small groups was a huge step, and even improved intimate relationships.

In that time I have only had two clients for whom power posing hasn't worked and both later admitted it was because they hadn't spent two minutes doing it. Have you got two minutes to change how others perceive you?

PRACTISE THE PHYSIOLOGY OF CONFIDENCE

Dr Cuddy provides us with a clear guide to the physiology of high-and low-power poses. As you read this section, firstly notice how you are sitting and which pose you are adopting naturally. As I describe the high-and low-power poses, shift your physiology accordingly.

Low-power poses will typically include an individual making themselves smaller and folding their hands and arms across themselves. Their heads will often be down and their shoulders will be up. If they are sitting their legs will typically be crossed quite tightly. You may occasionally see someone touching their neck. All of these combine to make the individual smaller and feel more protected.

High-power poses help the individual look bigger and more open. Typically hands or arms will be stretched out or open (imagine someone sitting with their hands clasped behind their head and with the elbows out either side of their head). Legs will be outstretched or open and if you adopt a power pose your head will be up. If you are exploring this now, find the most comfortable or natural position that you can stand while filling the largest space possible.

It is important to observe these gestures in clusters. In other words if you notice someone sitting with their arms folded please do not assume they are in a low-power pose. Look for groups of gestures and when adopting the power pose yourself demonstrate as many of the gestures as possible.

DECIDE WHEN TO POWER POSE

What is clear from Dr Cuddy's work and my experience is that the best time to use the power pose is not during an event when you want to feel high in power and low in stress but some time just before the event.

When preparing for an important meeting for example, spending two minutes in a small private space in your best power pose will get the desired result. Think for a moment in which areas of your life this would be most useful for you.

Since studying power posing many of my clients have used it to prepare for interviews, presentations, disciplinary reviews, business dinners, first dates and even to support a partner through labour!

On occasion it may be helpful to adopt a power pose live. This will typically be in a situation where another person is trying to be dominant and you want to respond in an equally dominant way. It is vital to choose these occasions carefully so as not to appear overpowering. A useful example is in a negotiation situation. In most cases I don't think it is the most desirable way to take control of the situation. My preference would be for you to use the power pose before the conversation then aim to build rapport with the other party during it. However if you find that the other party is being deliberately dominating and challenging during a negotiation then adopting a powerful physiology could be a valuable step to maintaining control.

FAKE IT UNTIL YOU BECOME IT

If you have read the early chapters of this book you will appreciate that the brain doesn't distinguish between what is real and what is made up. This means that all states are real, whether we have triggered them consciously or they have happened naturally. Cuddy underlines this in her work. She states that by using the power pose you aren't being something different but instead showing up as a better version of your natural self. You are also setting the foundations for that confident, powerful state to become a default state for you.

Try this experiment over the next month. Choose a specific situation that makes you feel out of place. It may be something simple like walking into a certain room or meeting or it may be when you meet with someone who you find slightly intimidating. For the next month ensure that before each of your chosen situations you adopt a power pose for a minimum of two minutes. After a month of doing this notice how you feel in these situations. My experience is that you suddenly realize that you feel different, less stressed and in greater control of the situation.

Putting it all together

Harvard University research has indicated that effective leaders characteristically have high testosterone and low cortisol. This chemical combination provides them with a platform upon which they are more assertive, more confident and more optimistic. They are willing to take more risks and make better decisions. The great news is that through the work of Dr Cuddy you are able to learn a technique which allows you to access this version of confidence in just two minutes. Through observing and carrying out controlled studies the team were able to establish that adopting high-power poses for just 120 seconds will lower the stress hormone (cortisol) and increase the dominance hormone (testosterone). Power poses are characterized by an open stance that fills the space around you. Your head will be up and your back straight.

The beauty of this research is that it adds more evidence and understanding to the principle that confidence is just a state which can be triggered at any time. It also confirms that by doing this on a regular basis this state becomes more of a default and changes our perspective on ourselves and the situations that we find ourselves in.

I can't recommend Dr Cuddy's TED Talk highly enough (see Further reading for a link to this talk). I will leave the final words of this chapter to her:

So I want to ask you first … both to try power posing and also I want to ask you to share the science, because this is simple. I don't have ego involved in this. Give it away. Share it with people, because the people who can use it the most are the ones with no resources and no technology and no status and no power. Give it to them because they can do it in private. They need their body's privacy and two minutes can significantly change the outcomes of their life.

Dr Cuddy

24 The language of confidence

❝ *Words are, of course, the most powerful drug used by mankind.* Rudyard Kipling

❝ *But if thought corrupts language, language can also corrupt thought.* George Orwell

❝ *The beginning of wisdom is the definition of terms.* Socrates

❝ *Without knowing the force of words, it is impossible to know more.* Confucius

❝ *Whatever words we utter should be chosen with care for people will hear them and be influenced by them for good or ill.* Buddha

Have you ever noticed that highly confident people seem to capture moods with nothing more than a few well-placed words? The language of the highly confident is specific and consistent in its make-up. Most importantly, for the context of this book, is that their language patterns can be learned and replicated.

Confident language is concise and simple. It is specific and engages those responding to it quickly. When highly confident people make requests they are very clear on what they want and spend much less time talking about what they don't want.

It is important to understand that the words and phrases we use every day become one of the fundamental frameworks through which we perceive the world around us. If your language tends to be negative or problem-focused then you will programme your brain to notice more negativity and problems. If your language is more positive and resourceful this becomes a filter for what you notice in the world.

This is particularly important for self-image and self-perception. If you consistently talk about yourself in negative terms and describe your shortcomings in detail, then this creates that self-image regardless of how accurate it is. I often notice people being particularly good at describing their negative traits while speaking with energy and positivity about the strengths of those around them. Does this sound like you? If so, a greater awareness of your language will have a big and positive impact on your confidence. The impact of language spreads beyond the individual though. The culture of a team or organization is influenced significantly by the language of its constituents. Leaders and senior managers in particular must be acutely aware of the influence of their language patterns.

This chapter focuses on three strategies that will help you to feel more confident and those around you to perceive you as more self-assured. As with many other techniques they require some practice to change programmes and patterns that have been natural to you for many years, but stick with it as the impact is significant. In particular the degree to which you are able to influence others around to your way of thinking will increase dramatically.

SAY WHAT YOU WANT, NOT WHAT YOU DON'T WANT

Your brain is fundamentally wired to follow commands that it is given. While we have built-in safeguards to consciously choose what we do, the brain, when given a task or instruction, has a natural propensity to follow that task or instruction.

This basic wiring underpins this strategy. For example if you say, internally or externally, that you 'don't want to be scared about presenting at conferences', your brain receives this message but deletes the 'don't'. You are programming yourself to be more scared about presenting at conferences.

As you explain to a friend that you always look terrible when you are dressed for a night out you are programming your brain to notice more of what you don't like when you are ready to go out.

Use language which helps you and others focus more on what you want rather than what you don't. Here are a few examples:

- Instead of 'I am tired' say 'I'm really looking forward to a good night's sleep'.
- Instead of 'I am stressed' say 'I really need to relax'.
- Instead of 'I am terrible at this' say 'I need to get better at this'.

This is not meant to be fluffy or blandly positive. Instead it is taking advantage of your brain's natural wiring to focus on getting more of what you want rather than what you don't.

REQUEST WHAT YOU WANT FROM OTHERS

This 'towards' language can be extended to your influence on others. In fact, you do this already you just don't realize it. I recently observed a new client addressing his management team. He started his presentation by saying, 'I don't want you to be nervous about the messages I am about to share with you' (the room shuffled at this point) 'I am going to present some figures and don't worry about the fact that you might find them complicated. I know for some it might be a little bit boring but if you try not to drift off or get confused we'll get there in the end'. Hardly inspirational stuff!

When you are influencing others, choose your words carefully to increase the chances of them doing what you want not what you don't.

Here are some examples:

- Instead of 'I don't want you to worry about what I'm asking you to do' say, 'I want you to feel relaxed about what I'm asking you to do'.
- Instead of 'Don't focus on the things that have gone wrong' say, 'Focus more on what has gone well'.
- Instead of 'If we lack focus we will lose' say, 'If we focus, we will win'.

Notice that in each of these examples the message is exactly the same but positioned in a way that gives the greatest chance to focus on what is needed. Use this towards approach to influence how others feel and their likelihood to complete the task as you would like.

USE MULTI-SENSORY LANGUAGE

Memories are created in a multi-sensory way. The more rich and multi-sensory the experience, the more multi-faceted and therefore powerful the memory you will create. We can contribute to this by using multi-sensory language in conversations with others. This is particularly useful when we are making presentations or pitches that we have a chance to prepare and rehearse.

In your audience you will have people who have a preference to think and remember in pictures. Others have a preference to think and remember sounds or auditory triggers. Another section of your audience will remember the feeling that is created during a memory most of all. If you use a range of visual, hearing and feeling or movement words in your communication it will be more memorable. The more memorable it is the more confident you will be perceived.

Take a look at these two extracts from Martin Luther King's famous 'I have a dream' speech. You will notice that it is littered with seeing, hearing and feeling words and phrases.

'Let us not wallow in the valley of despair. I say to you today my friends – so even though we face the difficulties of today and tomorrow, I still have a dream. It is a dream deeply rooted in the American dream.

I have a dream that one day this nation will rise up and live out the true meaning of its creed: 'We hold these truths to be self-evident, that all men are created equal.'

I have a dream that one day on the red hills of Georgia the sons of former slaves and the sons of former slave owners will be able to sit down together at the table of brotherhood.

I have a dream that one day even the state of Mississippi, a state sweltering with the heat of injustice, sweltering with the heat of oppression, will be transformed into an oasis of freedom and justice.

This will be the day, this will be the day when all of God's children will be able to sing with new meaning 'My country 'tis of thee, sweet land of liberty, of thee I sing. Land where my fathers died, land of the Pilgrim's pride, from every mountainside, let freedom ring!'

And if America is to be a great nation, this must become true. And so let freedom ring from the prodigious hilltops of New Hampshire. Let freedom ring from the mighty mountains of New York. Let freedom ring from the heightening Alleghenies of Pennsylvania.

Let freedom ring from the snow-capped Rockies of Colorado. Let freedom ring from the curvaceous slopes of California.

But not only that; let freedom ring from Stone Mountain of Georgia.

Let freedom ring from Lookout Mountain of Tennessee.

Let freedom ring from every hill and molehill of Mississippi – from every mountainside.'

The next time you plan a presentation or meeting, think about how you can use multi-sensory language even more to engage your audience.

Putting it all together

Many people don't pay attention to the words and phrases that they use day in and day out, but your language is a significant factor in your self-confidence and others' perception of how confident you are.

Highly confident people use more 'towards language' describing what they want rather than what they don't. This helps a huge amount as our brains are built to follow commands but don't easily recognize words like 'don't'. If you tell yourself, 'Don't worry about what other people think', you will delete the first word and focus much more on the rest of the command. A slight change in your internal language will make a huge difference.

This principle transfers easily to your communication with others. Using towards commands will increase your influence and therefore your confidence.

25 Creating a confident image

> *The most courageous act is still to think for yourself. Aloud.*
> Coco Chanel

> *I think the reward for conformity is that everyone likes you except yourself.* Rita Mae Brown

> *Always be a first rate version of yourself and not a second rate version of someone else.* Judy Garland

> *Don't you ever let a soul in the world tell you that you can't be exactly who you are.* Lady Gaga

> *I think everybody's weird. We should all celebrate our individuality and not be embarrassed or ashamed of it.* Johnny Depp

Too many people use image as a mask for a lack of confidence. This is not enough and will crack too easily. The hordes of young people changing their looks through needless and over-the-top plastic surgery is testament to this.

I do believe though that as you get the foundations of long-term and genuine confidence in place, your personal image and style should be a reflection and accelerator of it.

Jenny Bersin is the owner of Jenny B Style and Image Consultancy (www.jennybstyle.co.uk) and author of *Style, the Road to Freedom*. As well as one-to-one consultations she leads seminars on Perfecting Personal Effectiveness, Dressing for Success, Addressing Dressing and The Art of Fiscal Attraction. Here is her expert view on creating a confident image.

Creating an effective confident personal image is as relevant in our private lives as it is in what we choose to do for a living. Most importantly, developing a look that speaks positively of who we are gives us the opportunity to know ourselves, like ourselves and to our own selves be true. It is about speaking clearly without saying a word.

Having a perfectly clear style strategy gives us a real opportunity to be ourselves, and to present ourselves, in the way that we wish. To have an image that works well for us. To quote Gore Vidal: 'Style is knowing who you are, what you want to say and not giving a damn.

Many of us confuse fashion with style. Fashion is a need to be identified by the labels that are worn and to be part of a crowd, however elite. Style is about shining through as an individual and is about using dress and demeanour as a celebration and an expression of who we are.

Difficulties arise in finding an image that expresses confidence when we have little, or no, direction – we need a clear and precise strategy.

Developing such a strategy gives us the chance to look at where we are and where we want to be; to signal who we are effectively and powerfully and manoeuvre change in a way that suits ourselves. Here's how:

KNOW THE IMPACT OF FIRST IMPRESSIONS

When you meet someone new it takes just three seconds for you to make that indelible first impression. With just a glance, you evaluate them. Two things happen so quickly they could almost be as one. Firstly, you notice the quality and level of energy they give out, whether they are open or closed, charming or alarming. Secondly, you respond to how they look, from their grooming to what they are wearing … and they do the same to you!

In those same three seconds, they have appraised your visual and behavioural appearance from head to toe. They have instantly analysed your dress, mannerisms and body language. You may intrigue some and disenchant others, but you will always rouse feelings in others. If they like what they see they will unconsciously tend to see the best in you and look for opportunities to say 'yes'. If they don't like what they see, the opposite is true.

Then, inside a further 87 seconds, without you having said a word, you have been appraised and decisions have been made about how good you are at your job, what your social standing is, how educated you are and how much you can be trusted. It will take six months for those first impressions to be changed.

What is the first impression that you want to create as you think about the immediacy of the impact you create? Does your current style reflect how you see yourself or how you want others to see you?

CHOOSE WHETHER TO TEASE OR PLEASE

Those who *tease* are generally of the opinion that others must take them as they find them. They may look dishevelled, disorganized and drab, but beneath they are a powerhouse of vibrancy, intelligence and diligence. They leave it to those whom they meet to be amazed and delighted when they discover the real person who lies below that dreary and unpromising surface!

Research shows that how you look affects not only how you feel about yourself but how others feel about you too. And, apparently, those who are successful not only increase their earning power but also the confidence that they have in themselves, whether at home, work or play.

Those who *please* take an easier route. Designers and creators make it their business (because it is their business!) to look as though they have flair, originality and inspired thought, whereas teachers and solicitors meet the needs of their clients by looking dependable, honest and with integrity. If they don't, those whom they meet may find it difficult to believe that they are good at what they do and worth listening to or employing.

An example, I am working with a client whose job is to guide and support senior managers into creating and effecting change within their businesses. Her role is one that is both inspirational and challenging. In terms of experience and intellect she is extremely able, BUT she sees a yawning gap. While her deeds and demeanour are spot-on her dress falls short. During her first consultation she described her choice of work dress as 'conforming, corporate, and dull'. Where does she want to be? 'Confident, self-assured, chic, original.' Easy enough to do now that she has recognized where she is and where she would like to be.

Do you want to tease or please with your personal style? Do you take an approach that is appropriate for your life and career now? Does your current wardrobe and style reflect this? How could you develop your approach further to make an even more confident statement?

DEVELOP YOUR IMAGE STRATEGY

When you look good you inspire those who you meet to have confidence in your skills. The more inspired they are, the more confident you become. The more confident you become, the more you inspire others to recognize you as a positive presence in their lives. You have clinched the art of being in demand. Being in demand will mean that you are more likely to be in a position to pick the job you want, the friends you want, the lifestyle you want.

Trying to find your own personal image is liberating. And, icing on the cake, get it right and you could be earning 8–20% more than your competitors who don't.

All you need is a simple strategy based on self-acceptance not self-criticism.

The mantra that I use with my clients is this:

SAY … STYLE PERSONALITY … SHAPE … SCALE and PROPORTION … SHADE

Understand it, implement it and you'll find developing your own effective personal style easy and effortless. Some of those who do it now … Michelle Obama, Aung San Suu Kyi, Brian Cox, and Bob Geldof.

These are not necessarily conventionally beautiful people but they are people with direction and focus who speak about who they are and what they are and what is important to them not only in their deeds, but in their dress and demeanour too. We do not need to speak to them to know this.

If you accepted who you are completely now, what would your style be? If your style really did create the first part of the impression you want others to have about you what would it be like? What changes do you need to make?'

Putting it all together

Jenny's strategies, as outlined here, should be part of the circle of confidence. As you develop that deep sense of confidence, then your image should magnify that. As it magnifies that growing inner confidence the feedback you will get from people around you will add further weight to your confidence.

From the very beginning of this book I have made it clear that confidence must start from within. It is something you do, not something you have, and while some of the strategies are external, all are designed to anchor this true inner state of confidence. The approach to your inner style must be the same. Style is something that develops from the inside-out. The image that you want to create for the outside world must be a reflection of how you see yourself. If you just work on creating the external world without paying attention to how congruent this is, it will create a shell-like style that will break easily and at the worst possible time.

If you pay a little attention to your style by answering the questions posed in this chapter, you are likely to find that it becomes effortless for you. As Graeme Fidler formerly of Ralph Lauren, Aquascutum and Bally, said: 'Fashion you can buy – style is inherent.'

26 Confidence from others

> **"** Don't let people disrespect you. My mom says don't open the door to the devil. Surround yourself with positive people.
> Cuba Gooding Jr

> **"** Look at people for an example, but then make sure to do things your way. Surround yourself with positive people.
> Queen Latifah

> **"** Be so good they can't ignore you. Steve Martin

> **"** Believe you can and you're halfway there. Theodore Roosevelt

> **"** I have insecurities of course, but I don't hang out with anyone who points them out to me. Adele

How many people can you think of who exude confidence? Who in your social network already demonstrates the characteristics of someone who is genuinely confident in a range of situations? The good news is that with a bit of study and attention you can begin to borrow their confidence traits and add them to your own.

When I deliver training sessions in confidence for mangers in sport and business, one of the things that I ask them to do is to analyse the characteristics of the most confident person that they know. Two things become really clear, really quickly. The first is that even though the individuals in the group tend to pick different people, many of the traits are very similar. Secondly, the traits are very easy to copy. When I then ask the people I am working with to consciously adopt the confidence traits that they have seen in others they find that it activates their own state of confidence. Even when they are put in a pressurized situation, like making an unprepared presentation to their fellow group members, they are able to do it in a much more assured manner when they also maintain the characteristics of their confidence mentors.

One reason for the success of these strategies relates back to a point made earlier in this book. Our brain doesn't differentiate easily between what is real and what is strongly imagined. When you adopt the traits of someone who you consider to be confident, your brain reacts to this as if the confidence is your own and happening naturally. It is useful to keep this fundamental brain wiring in place as you read through the practical strategies in this chapter and plan how you will use them.

NOTICE HOW THEY WALK INTO A ROOM

If you want to learn from the confidence of others, then analysis of their entrance into a room is a great place to start. There are some very definite patterns in how a confident person holds themselves as they enter a new environment. Pay close attention to their posture and in particular the level of their head. Scrutinize their eye contact and how they scan the room as they enter. Notice their facial expressions as they walk in and as they settle in the room. Observe the pace that they walk in at and how they sit or stand in their chosen position. The more attention you pay, the more detail you will notice. One of the things that I often look for is tension in the muscles around the jawline and eyes. This might not be something you will immediately notice, but over time it becomes very observable.

How the confident enter a room is also a metaphor for how they fill any particular space. Highly confident people seem to have a presence even if they aren't doing much. I've heard it described as an aura or energy. They just have something that brings people's attention to them which has nothing to do with how they are dressed or their physique. If this is true for the confident people who are unknowingly mentoring you, then look out for this. With attention you will notice certain things that they do which generate this quality.

MIND THEIR LANGUAGE

I would also highly recommend that you pay attention to the language patterns of your chosen subject and try them on for yourself. In Chapter 24 we looked specifically at language and building your own patterns, but modelling the patterns of others is a great place to start.

Here are some patterns to look out for:

- Do they use language that focuses on what they want or what they don't want?
- Do they spend more time talking about what has gone well or about recent failures?
- Do they have any specific verbal tics?
- How natural is their tone and their accent?
- What do you notice about their volume and pace?
- Do they pause little or often?

The aim is not to mimic them exactly but to try the patterns of language that you think create the sense of confidence in them or others. This is especially powerful if you can model the language patterns of a range of people who are confident in varying situations. The traits that are most consistent are likely to be the ones that are most important so experiment with them first.

BUILD A CONFIDENT NETWORK

While observing and modelling your confident exemplar it is really valuable to notice the people who they spend most time with. Many years ago Jim Rohn, the personal development guru, suggested that your income is likely to be an average of the incomes of the five people that you spend most time with. While I'm not sure the maths works perfectly, I think the concept is a healthy one to adopt and it lends itself perfectly to confidence. I am sure as you notice your exemplar's peer group it will be apparent that they do not feed their confidence by surrounding themselves with people who have less confidence than them. The opposite is almost always true: confident people tend to have social and business networks filled with people who are equally confident and often contain people who are even more certain of themselves.

Study how they operate in their networks and how they build them. When I am doing this kind of observation, there are small nuances to their strategies that I wouldn't have thought of which make all the difference when I apply them. One example of this came from my friend and ex-colleague Steve Marriott. Steve is an expert business coach and was in the service of a client modelling a brilliant business networker. This individual had a reputation for being the most connected person at any business event and met everyone with a confidence and certainty that left others in the shade. When Steve explored her strategies for making connections there was one very simple tactic that made a huge difference. She was always the first to arrive at an event and the last to leave. Simple as this may sound, it meant she was more likely to meet and spend quality time meeting more people. Steve passed this insight onto his clients and applied it himself with huge success.

The insight you gain may not be quite so straightforward but as in the previous strategy the more you pay attention the more that you will notice.

Putting it all together

No matter what walk of life you are from, you are surrounded by people who demonstrate genuine confidence. Whether this is at work, in your social life or even in the media, you have confident exemplars all around you. Whether the traits that highly confident people demonstrate are consciously created or have evolved over time, they still achieve the same end result. Your job in your journey to become consistently confident is to observe and explore these characteristics and experiment with them for yourself.

There are only two ways that this kind of modelling doesn't work. The first is if you do the observation and don't apply it. I have worked with clients for whom the exploration was a means to an end. Simply watching the confident person can have an impact on your state, but experimenting with applying the strategies is the jumpstart to awakening your own state of confidence. The second obstacle comes if you wait until you're in a pressurized situation to experiment with applying the strategies you've observed in others. For example, if you notice specific language patterns, try them out in situations where it doesn't matter if they don't trip off your tongue in the way that you would like.

Finally for this chapter I can't recommend enough surrounding yourself with confident people who you can learn from. It can be uncomfortable at first, but those with genuine confidence (rather than surface arrogance) should not be overwhelming. The more comfortable you are around the confident the higher your default level of confidence will be.

27 Make confident decisions

66 *Freedom is the opportunity to make decisions.* Kenneth Hildebrand

66 *The hardest thing to learn in life is which bridge to cross and which to burn.* David Russell

66 *The indispensable first step to getting the things you want out of life is this: decide what you want.* Ben Stein

66 *The value of decisions depends upon the courage required to render them.* Napoleon Hill

66 *We know what happens to people who stay in the middle of the road. They get run over.* Aneurin Bevan

Twelve frogs are idling the day away in a garden pond, each sitting on their own lily pad. Five decide to jump into the water. How many frogs are left sitting on lily pads?

If you've heard this little riddle before or are particularly astute today, you will know the answer is twelve. That's because while five frogs decided to jump, none of them actually did it! And herein lies the two parts of a confident decision.

1. Confidence in deciding what you want or need to do.
2. Confidence to follow through on your decision by taking action.

While still considering the options or possibilities open to you when taking an important decision (part one), you can put yourself under huge amounts of unnecessary pressure to take immediate action. This clouds your thinking and blocks your creativity. If you were eavesdropping on a conversation between these frogs you might hear things like:

'I've been thinking about what I should do all day and I still haven't done anything. All of the other frogs know what to do. If I don't make a decision soon, I must be a bad frog.'

Sometimes we already know what to do, yet we spend hours creating good and bad scenarios in our head of the decision playing out. It is like we are a fortune teller with a remote-controlled crystal ball where we can change the outcome again and again at the touch of a button. We become exhausted purely by the thought of taking action. These frogs might be saying things like:

'I had my frog-fingers burnt last year when I went for a swim and someone stole my lily pad. I've taken action too quickly in the past without thinking things through. I'll just stay here a bit longer.'

While your decisions don't often involve frogs, you might see similarities or patterns in the decisions you've needed to make in the past.

I have worked with many clients who wanted help with an important decision and report feeling 'a bit stuck'. Some even admit they can never make a decision, or at least it seems that way to them. On these occasions a breakthrough almost always occurs when we separate and explore each of these two parts.

We are all capable of making brilliant decisions and we do so in our own unique way. There are times when it can be useful to get a helping hand along the way to make a confident decision.

RELEASE THE PRESSURE VALVE TO YOUR DECISION

If we are in a building and hear the sound of the fire alarm, or we see someone about to put themselves in immediate danger, the situation dictates that we take immediate action. We all have an in-built mechanism that kicks in and spurs us into action, without thinking some might say. Of course in reality there is a huge amount of sophisticated neural function taking place in these moments. This includes diverting our inner resources away from 'logical reasoning' to the more primal 'fight or flight' response.

In most situations, however, we can afford a period of time to generate and assess options available to us without serious consequences. The fact that we can give ourselves permission to do so, with the pressure of action removed, can make us so much more resourceful, creative and empowered while we decide what to do.

Sometimes I will ask a client to go away and consider their decision for a whole week. The only rule is that they are not allowed to take any action at all during that week. Even if they become certain about their decision, and it is safe to do so, they must not act upon it. Invariably they come back with much greater clarity and tell me what they want to do.

This period of pressure-free time might be ten minutes during an important business meeting, 24 hours while a big-ticket is on special-offer or a week while you decide to ask for your partner's hand in marriage. You can create a period of time to research, reflect, ask advice, or simply let go and relax for a while. Whatever is right for you in that moment, you create space to generate options and make a confident decision.

Theodore C. Sorensen, advisor to John F Kennedy and author of *Decision-Making in the White House* said: 'And once I have all the options before me, then I comfortably and confidently make my decision'.

MAKE DECISIONS USING THE HEART, HEAD AND GUT

One of the most useful ways I have found to explore a decision has been developed from an exercise in Michael Neill's brilliant book *You Can Have What You Want*. Neill suggests using your head, heart and gut when exploring something important. Here are some questions that can help you. You might want to add some of your own too.

Use your head!

- Who has successfully made a similar decision before?
- What would the expert in this area advise?
- Where can you find more information?

Listen to your heart!

- What is the kindest thing to do right now?
- What would your guardian angel tell you to do?
- If you were living completely by your values, what would you do?

Trust your gut!

- What do you instinctively know to do already?
- What do you feel is right for you now?
- If a miracle happened overnight and the decision was already made, what would it be?

So you have created space without the pressure to act and generated options from which you can comfortably and confidently make your decision. When you reach the end of the period of time you've allowed, or circumstances change, then it is time to make your decision. And choose when to act.

KNOW WHEN TO ACT

So you have now made a decision, but there is still the matter of acting upon it. In his book *Think and Grow Rich*, Napoleon Hill says 'Successful people make decisions quickly, and change them very slowly, if and when they change them at all. Yes, people who make decisions go to the top. And those who don't make decisions seem to go nowhere.'

I believe the successful people Hill talks about are those who act upon their decisions. They have confidence that the conditions, circumstances and consequences are right for them to act. There are also some less-successful people who may have also made good decisions but unless they act upon them to the outside world they appear not to have decided anything.

Many people have a high setting for certainty in their lives. Doing anything that is unfamiliar or out of the ordinary can feel uncomfortable. When taking action on the back of a decision we can sometimes look for a 100 per cent guarantee that things will work out as we desire. And, of course, we can't see into the future and few outcomes can be 100 per cent guaranteed. Sometimes we will gain and there are times we might lose. All we can do is trust that we make the best decisions we can with the resources we have.

As a final test of a decision, I sometimes find the following exercise really useful to explore.

Draw a four-block grid (a large square divided into four smaller squares). Give the top left-hand square the title DO & GAIN. In that square write down what you expect to gain by taking action. Now title the bottom-left square DO & LOSE and write down the things you might lose by taking action.

The two squares to the right-hand side are to explore what you might lose or gain by not taking action. Title the top-right square DON'T & GAIN and write down what you could gain from doing nothing. Finally title the bottom-right square DON'T & LOSE and write down what you might lose from doing nothing.

One of the things this exercise can remind us is that we nearly always have complete choice of when to act upon an important decision. It also helps us ensure the time is right to act.

Putting it all together

Theodore Roosevelt once said: 'In a moment of decision, the best thing you can do is the right thing to do. The worst thing you can do is nothing.'

A confident decision comes in two parts: deciding what to do and when to take action. Taking time to generate options without the pressure to act is doing something.

Successful people know that a successful decision comes with action when the time is right and conditions are right. They know they can't predict the future and they know they won't get it right every time. They learn to trust in their ability to make good decisions.

28 Make more decisions

> **66** Once a decision was made, I didn't worry about it afterward.
> Harry S. Truman

> **66** Big decisions in my life have always come easy and are made
> without hesitation. It is easier for me to make a life-changing
> decision than to decide what to get for dessert. Tony Hawk

> **66** Some people want it to happen, some wish it would happen,
> others make it happen. Michael Jordan

> **66** I think it's very important that you make your own decision
> about what you are. Therefore you're responsible for your
> actions, so you don't blame other people. Prince William

> **66** There is no decision that we can make that doesn't come with
> some sort of balance or sacrifice. Simon Sinek

What makes a good decision-maker? When working with
developing leaders I ask this question regularly and the
responses range from the ability to never be wrong through to
assumptions about the pace of the decision-maker in processing
information. While the quality of decision-making is largely judged
retrospectively it is clear that confident decision-makers are
comfortable making more decisions more quickly. In Chapter 27 we
shared the techniques that the highly confident use to make good
decisions by understanding how they make them. In this chapter
we explore how the highly confident make quicker decisions.
Combining your learning from these two chapters provides a
powerful platform to build confidence, presence and gravitas in a
range of situations and circumstances.

I often consider decision-making to be the bridge between ideas and action. You can have the best ideas, but if you take too long to cross the bridge your energy to follow that through will disappear. While I am an advocate of taking action (see Chapter 29 Take action), pacey decision-making will ensure those actions are well placed and add value to the situation.

Fast decision-making is not a lack of fear about getting things wrong. Simply, highly confident people have developed the ability to hedge their decisions. When the risk is low they tend to make quicker decisions with minimum information required. Larger decisions require more thinking but still rely more on intuition than details. Decisions that have a wider impact or greater repercussions are well considered and rely more heavily on evidence and experience. As with action-orientation it can be useful to consider decision-making as a muscle to be developed. The more you work the muscle the better it will perform. As you exercise it and stretch it the more it will build. Do not wait until a crucial life decision presents itself to develop your decision-making.

CHOOSE FROM THE MENU QUICKLY

When you eat out how do you choose your food? Do you review every option available on the menu imagining how each will look, taste and smell? Do you confer with each of your party to find out what they are having before going back to the menu again and restarting the process?

Choosing from the menu at your favourite eatery should be an enjoyable and low-risk decision. So why not speed up the process? Richard Bandler, the co-creator of Neuro-Linguistic Programming, is reputed to have a simple process for choosing from any menu. He will read down the menu until he finds something he likes and he chooses that without reading any further. Simple!

This decision-making approach is simple, useful and leaves more time for the really important things (in this case socializing). I highly recommend it. Of course the approach spreads much further than choosing food. What are the other low-risk areas of your life you can stop over-thinking and make quicker decisions in?

Here are some examples:

- Choosing between two items of clothing you want to buy. If you like them both, just pick one.
- Deciding where to go on holiday. If they all seem great just choose the one that comes first in the alphabet.
- Which task to do first. If they are equally important just do one.
- What drink to have during a night out. If you like them all, just pick the first one that comes to mind; you can always have a different one next.

These may all seem like trivial examples, but that is the point. If it isn't a big decision use it as a training ground for making decisions quickly.

CHOOSE WHAT'S NOT ON THE MENU

Let's head off to your favourite eatery again and consider another way to choose what to eat. How often do you stop and ask yourself what you would really like before you even look at the menu? Most of us are conditioned by the assumption that we can only have what we think is available. How often do you ask for something that isn't on the menu? Try it, you will be surprised how often restaurants are able to provide or create what you want.

Now think of how this simple principle of ordering 'off the menu' can apply in other areas of your life. A great example is in career decisions. I have coached many people over the years who are struggling with decisions about what they should do next. Typically the choice is between two roles that are really what they want. It is rare for people to scope out their ideal job. Being clear on what your perfect role looks like speeds up the decision-making process considerably.

Michael Neill, the renowned success coach, once gave me a coaching assignment which entailed making decisions based on only one criterion – what do I want to do now? It was fascinating both to notice my reaction to the assignment and the result.

My initial reaction was resistance. 'I can't possibly do that, it will never work' was the primary pushback. Once I realized that I was sensible, trustworthy and reasonably sane, I understood that I wouldn't ruin my life during a week of doing this. The results of the assignment were that I was able to make more decisions and be more productive. Even tasks that I had been putting off for weeks got done. The difference was that I chose to do them and felt good about it rather than feeling that I should do them and procrastinating.

I would highly recommend the experiment. If you feel unsure about whether you can trust yourself to do the right thing, use it in prioritizing your work. I am sure you will find that you can trust yourself to make more decisions without the usual turmoil.

REDEFINE BAD DECISIONS

Let us take one last visit to that restaurant. You have chosen quickly, either from the menu or off the menu. Your food arrives and you tuck in. After a few mouthfuls the disappointment sets in. It's just not quite hitting the spot. Having eaten as much as you can, you push the half-eaten meal away. My question is: does this make the original decision a bad one?

All too often I see people damaging their confidence by chastising themselves over perfectly good decisions that then haven't worked out. 'I always make bad decisions' is a familiar cry from those low on genuine confidence. Highly confident people have a different set of criteria for what makes decisions good or bad. Their focus is on the process not the outcome.

If you have made a decision in the right way and for the right reason, then that is a good decision regardless of the outcome. For example if you take a new job because the career prospects are better, the organization has a good record of staff development and you get a positive feeling for your new manager, then that is a great decision. If you don't like the job and the promises about your career prove to be false, that doesn't make the decision a bad one, it makes the company a bad one.

Consider how you define good and bad decisions. Is it on process or outcome? Reflect on key decisions that you have made over the past year and categorize them based on the quality and pace of decision-making rather than the outcome alone.

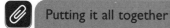

In my early twenties, I found myself in a long-term relationship that was proving unfulfilling for me. I couldn't decide whether that lack of fulfilment lay with me or my partner. She was a good person but not right for me, but at the same time I had changed and wasn't nurturing the relationship to give it the chance to grow with me. I needed to make a big decision that would define the course of my life for many years to come.

Choice one was to dedicate myself to my partner and that relationship. It would need energy, patience, understanding and sacrifice. If that was the road I was going to take, it needed to be for the long haul. The relationship would not be repaired overnight.

Choice two was to let it go. We had been together from a young age and, as difficult and scary as it felt, perhaps a fresh start would be best for both of us. Over many months I explored the options. At times I thought I had made a decision and changed my mind when it came to committing to it. I made pros and cons lists that explored every option I could conceive and despite every sensible approach to the decision I could take, I just couldn't settle.

Ultimately the five-year relationship ended on the toss of a coin. From that moment on I vowed that I would improve the pace that I made decisions at. Not because I couldn't decide, but because I really knew the decision that needed to be made but couldn't commit to it. Highly confident people make decisions quickly and well. When they have explored what they need to they commit without ever worrying about the implications of a wrong decision.

In decision-making, hindsight is rarely a helpful thing. It can fool you into thinking badly-made decisions were good ones and well thought-through decisions were bad. A well developed decision-making muscle will help you make better decisions more quickly, easily and confidently.

(29) Take action

When it is obvious that the goals cannot be reached, don't adjust the goals, adjust the action steps. Confucius

In order to carry a positive action we must develop here a positive vision. Dalai Lama

Action is the foundational key to all success. Pablo Picasso

You are what you do, not what you say you'll do. C.G. Jung

If you're going to be able to look back on something and laugh about it, you might as well laugh about it now. Marie Osmond

We have already explored the fact that confidence isn't something that we have or don't have. In Chapter 1 we introduced the idea that confidence is a state. It is something that we feel at certain times and don't feel at other times and, in that respect, we can look at confidence as something that we 'do' or 'don't do'.

The actual word 'do' is a verb that is defined as performing a particular task or working on something specific. It's interesting to see that word 'state' appears in the the *Oxford English Dictionary* definition of the word: 'do': 'Do…Work on (something) to bring it to completion or to a required state'.

In order to 'do confidence' you therefore need to take action orientated towards achieving the desired outcome, the state of confidence.

Learning to access a confident state should be tackled in exactly the same way as you would tackle any big project – by breaking it down into small, bite-sized goals.

Simply saying 'I want to be more confident' doesn't provide a clear enough goal for us to work towards. More confident when? More confident in what situations? What does more confident look like?

You could use the approaches in Chapter 17 (goal-setting) to do this in a way that really works for you.

Once you have these defined, get quickly into action. I have met many talented people who haven't achieved what they should have done because they didn't take action. Procrastination is the enemy of confidence. Don't hang around, do something! To quote Norman Peale: 'Action is a great restorer and builder of confidence. Inaction is not only the result, but the cause, of fear. Perhaps the action you take will be successful; perhaps different action or adjustments will have to follow. But any action is better than no action at all.'

STRETCH YOURSELF

There are many times in your life when you will have experienced a confident state. This may have been at a particular time, with certain groups of people, completing a set activity or perhaps in a specific environment. But you probably didn't feel confident the very first time you were in this situation.

Consider the analogy of driving a car. The very first time you stepped into a car for your first driving lesson I suspect that you didn't feel particularly confident. The reason for this is that it was a new activity for you, which was probably pushing you into your 'stretch' zone, or perhaps even your 'panic' zone. If it pushed you into your panic zone then you will have struggled to adapt and learn new skills. The reason for this is that it will have activated your primeval 'fight or flight' response deep within a part of the brain called the amygdala. In this heightened state of alert, your brain channels all of its resources towards survival. In doing so, it blocks out all other non-critical thoughts and processes. There will have been absolutely no learning taking place and you will have been in a far from confident state.

Equally, when you're within your comfort zone, very little learning takes place albeit for different reasons. Have you ever been driving along the motorway and suddenly thought to yourself, 'Where did the last ten miles go?'

The reason behind this common occurrence is that your brain is operating within in its comfort zone. Your brain is processing information with very little conscious thought.

KEEP DOING NEW THINGS

My colleague Ben Morton describes beautifully the importance of doing new things to help anchor our confidence:

'We generally tend to feel un-confident undertaking new activities or in new situations because they feel unfamiliar to us. By taking action, by taking small steps towards the very thing that makes us feel uncomfortable we are able to expand our comfort zone to encompass the "new thing". It will not provide us with an instant confidence transformation (although it may for some), but over time by consistently and repeatedly taking small, action-orientated steps we are able to expand our comfort zone.'

The key is to not beat ourselves up about the fact that we don't feel like the world's most confident person. Research by David Rock shows that among other basic human needs we also have a requirement for a sense of certainty and relatedness. Certainty is about knowing what is coming, how an event will turn out and what the outcomes will be. Relatedness is about our social needs, needing to feel connected to and accepted by those around us. Having these needs met activates a primary reward response in our brains and equally, not having them (or perceiving that we may not have them) activates a primary threat response.

DON'T LET UP

Consider for a moment the metaphor of a 'confidence muscle'. To strengthen a muscle we need to exercise it over and over again; in doing so it grows bigger and stronger. It is the same with confidence.

By repeating our small actions over and over again our brains begin to create new connections through a process known as neuro-plasticity, and in doing so, our comfort zone begins to expand.

Once you begin to feel more comfortable with the one action, you simply need to repeat the process. What is the next small action you could take to move you another step along the scale?

Accessing a more confident state is about taking consistent and repeated action. The reason that we can often feel un-confident is as a result of something being new, unfamiliar and outside of our comfort zone. One strategy to enable us to tap into a more confident state is, therefore, to take action. It is about turning towards the very thing that makes us feel un-confident and taking small, deliberate actions that will move us just one step closer to confident. And in doing so, we slowly but surely begin to expand our comfort zone until it completely encompasses the thing that once scared us the most.

Putting it all together

This is perhaps the simplest of all of the principles, but perhaps is the one that should be restated most often. Do something and keep doing things that take you in the direction that you want to go. Even if your action isn't quite on the right track then I strongly believe, as the metaphor goes, that it is easier to change the course of a ship that is moving than it is to get it moving in the first instance.

Stretching yourself out of your comfort zone creates a learning habit and a powerful one at that. A habit of finding new things to do programmes our brains to get certainty in new ways. Certainty for innovators often comes from the knowledge that they won't get it right first time rather than the desire to get it right first time. Once you have started these things then don't let up. Keep going and experimenting constantly. If you aren't naturally action-orientated then help reprogramme your brain to reduce the thinking time and increase the doing time.

(30) Financial confidence

❝ *All I ask is the chance to prove that money can't make me happy.* Spike Milligan

❝ *Sometimes your best investments are the ones you don't make.* Donald Trump

❝ *Anybody who thinks money will make you happy, hasn't got money.* David Geffen

❝ *When it is obvious that the goals cannot be reached, don't adjust the goals, adjust the action steps.* Confucius

❝ *In order to carry a positive action we must develop here a positive vision.* Dalai Lama

How connected are confidence and money in your life? Do you have more confidence the more money that you have? Many of us believe that the more wealth we have the happier and more confident we will become. My experience is that this generally isn't true. In this chapter I want to share with you some of the beliefs and strategies that the financially highly confident people I have encountered have about money and wealth. However I want to clearly steer you away from this as a starting point. Wealth and financial comfort comes as a result of mastering the strategies contained throughout the rest of this book. Confidence does not come as a result of a large bank balance.

Several years ago I carried out a study on happiness and found that, other than in the social group that had the lowest financial resources, there was no correlation between wealth and happiness. In addition those with a higher income often had less confidence in their financial position than those in the lower earning brackets. The important message is to ensure that you are anchoring confidence in every area of your life. You can then use these strategies for financial confidence as the icing on the cake.

Every financially confident person that I have worked with or studied shared an additional financial belief, strategy and behaviour. Each of them clearly demonstrated an abundance mentality. They made giving a fundamental part of their approach to money. One of the coaches I worked with would tithe one third of his gross income every month. This would be automatically taken from his account and not be part of his financial calculations. He started this practice when he earned a very modest income and continued through his business career even when he was earning a seven-figure sum. Indeed one of the things he credited to his increased wealth was his abundance mentality.

Before you even continue to the main strategies in this chapter think about how much you could give to those needier than you and how this may help to build your confidence in finance and life.

CHECK YOUR FINANCIAL THERMOMETER

How much would you have to have in order for you to consider yourself rich? £10,000? £100,000? £1,000,000? More importantly how much would you have to have in order to be completely financially free?

For many people the actual amount of money that they need to earn and save in order to be financially free on paper is much less than they think. We rarely think about it because we haven't consciously set our financial thermometer. In other words we aren't consciously aware of the settings on our internal belief system that tells us what too much and too little money is.

Stop for a moment and answer the following questions:

1. How much would you love to earn in a year?
2. If you checked your bank balance tomorrow, what figure would you be overjoyed to see in it?
3. How much do you think you deserve to earn this year?
4. What amount of money would be uncomfortably high to see in your bank account?

Your answers to questions 3 and 4 should be considerably higher than 1 and 2. If not then revisit your beliefs about money and work to increase the amount of money you would be comfortable with earning and having.

If you have a steady income and service any debt that you have, but still regularly worry about money, then take time to review objectively your financial status.

A great question to ask is: 'If you didn't earn another penny from this moment on, how long would it take before you were out on the street?' Most people's initial estimate significantly underestimates the reality. Take into account any savings you have, luxury items you could sell and money you could borrow from family and friends. If the length of time is three months or more, it is highly unlikely that you would ever find yourself in that position. You will have the skills, knowledge experience and network to find another job. With this insight you have the foundations of your financial confidence. Unless you plan to take big risks you are highly unlikely to end up penniless so you can examine your worries with a more objective viewpoint.

SPEND LESS THAN YOU EARN

This could win the prize for the simplest strategy in this book. It might be the easiest to understand, but it doesn't appear to be the easiest for people to implement. Now is a useful point to ask yourself the question: do you know the difference between the amount you earn and the amount you have to pay out each week? A highly successful financial advisor recently told me that very few people know their outgoings versus their income. Even those with higher incomes are prone to get into financial difficulties due to a lack of attention to the basics.

If you have become wrapped up in the current 'buy now pay later' culture, it is time to change the question that you ask yourself. Instead of asking, 'How can I get that outfit/phone/car etc?', the new question you must ask yourself to regain your financial confidence is, 'What is the best lifestyle that I can create on the income that I have?' Taking control of your spending doesn't mean that you don't get any treats; in fact it probably means the opposite. After a short period of time you will find that you are more mindful about spending and buy treats and luxuries that you appreciate most.

(There is a brilliant money saving expert website, with a great page specifically to help you save money, listed at the back under Further reading).

BUILD A MONEY MACHINE

One of the best approaches to increasing your financial confidence is to create a system that you know helps to grow the assets that you have. One of the most commonly touted by personal development experts is the 'three pots' approach to assigning your assets. This approach ensures that you take a balanced approach to saving and investment but one that allows you to grow your assets.

Out of the money that you have to invest you create three pots to allocate that money to.

The security pot

This is where you make investments that are secure by nature. These investments won't give a huge return but over the longer period the return grows. Your first investment must be into your security pot.

Typical security pot investments include:

- Cash (2–6 months' worth)
- Pension

- Life insurance
- Fixed bonds
- Government investments
- Your home

The growth pot

This is where you place your growth investments. These investments provide a much greater rate of return but have a much greater risk that the investment may not be successful. There is no guarantee of return on a growth investment.

The fantasy pot

These are the material things that you want for no other reason than it would be wonderful to have them. It could be a home in the sun, an executive box at your favourite sports venue, a second or third car. Essentially anything that you don't actually need but would love to have.

Typically if you are starting out on your investment journey, you may want to put around 40 per cent of your investment capital in the security pot and then split the rest between the growth and fantasy pots. Remember the more you put into your fantasy pot the less your return will be.

If you are older you may want to play it safe and put more in the security bucket, while if you're younger or more aggressive you might consider dropping the security pot to 30 per cent.

Your next step is to decide what the right balance is for you and, with the advice of an independent financial expert, decide on the right investments for you.

Putting it all together

High salaries and big bank balances do not guarantee confidence. However, as you are developing confidence in all other areas of your life, it is a great opportunity to insure against financial challenges that may make it more difficult to maintain your confidence levels.

The financial services industry is awash with advice and the fundamentals of being confident are not complicated. The crucial factor that is ignored by most financial experts is that your wealth and financial confidence is a direct reflection of your beliefs and relationship with wealth. Let me illustrate this with an example a coach shared with me following a conversation with a client.

He had worked with this client for some time and knew he was a highly successful businessman in Los Angeles. The businessman contacted him for an emergency coaching session. He asked the coach to advise him on how to convince his wife of the importance of a business deal he was about to embark on. He described to the coach how important the deal was and that if he didn't focus on it, it could jeopardize his whole business. His wife didn't understand this and was threatening to leave him if he went through with it. For a moment the coach was caught up in the story but then stopped his client to ask, 'If you didn't earn another cent from this day, how long would it take before you were out on the street?' The client paused thoughtfully before answering, 'Seven years'. When the coach probed a little further he revealed that his assets were in the high tens of millions of dollars.

My coach helped me realize at that point that our financial confidence does not shift with our bank balance. In fact, instead we must build our confidence in order to build our wealth.

31 Become the world's leading expert

> **''** You have to have confidence in your ability, and then be tough enough to follow through. Rosalynn Carter

> **''** Self-reverence, self-knowledge, self-control: These three alone lead life to sovereign power. Alfred Tennyson

> **''** Trust yourself. You know more than you think you do.
> Dr Benjamin Spock

> **''** It is your attitude, not your aptitude, that determines your altitude. Zig Ziglar

> **''** Ability may take you to the top, but it takes character to stay there. William Blake

My early steps into consultancy and coaching were tentative and nervous. My tender age and lack of formal qualifications left me in awe of colleagues and clients and with a consistent feeling of having to fake it until I made it. Few people had a greater role in my development in those early days than Patrick Hare. Not only was he one of the most intelligent and insightful people that I have ever met, he was also one of the most self-confident. He was brilliant and exemplified so much of what real genuine confidence brings. He also developed one of the most valuable confidence strategies that I have ever learned and used, and I am delighted to share it with you.

This strategy is perfect for those moments when you are put on the spot to answer a question that you haven't had the time to formulate an answer for. It will help you to remain calm, appear confident and to answer any question well. As you get comfortable with the process it is best to follow it precisely and in the order described in this chapter. When you are familiar with it you will refine it and find your own format.

I have one final note of caution before I share this strategy. I am aware that some people use this 'world's leading expert' to become a fantastic bluffer. This isn't what the strategy is designed for and, while it will help you to fly by the seat of your pants more convincingly, eventually you will be caught out. In a meeting when you are being challenged on facts, figures or data, if you really don't know then there is more confidence in calmly saying that you will need to confirm the information and come back to them than to completely guess. The world's leading expert strategy is better placed in situations where you are being asked your opinion or when you know the answer but can't bring it to mind.

MAKE EYE CONTACT AND STEP FORWARD

When people are nervous or put on the spot, one of the automatic physiological responses is to take a step back. This is a small socially acceptable version of our flight reaction kicking in. Nervousness also reduces our comfort with eye contact, again triggered by a reptilian response to look for other threats and escape routes. Understanding this makes sense of the first two stages of our strategy. When asked a question that you want to respond to in the way a world's leading expert would is to give full and relaxed eye contact as they ask the question. An old but valuable guide for good eye contact is to rotate your gaze within the triangle formed by the two eyes and mouth of the person you are connecting with.

As they finish asking the question, make a very small subtle movement towards them. For example if I am presenting to a group and one of the members asks a question, I take a small half-step towards them as I prepare to answer. If you are in a meeting where all participants are seated the movement may be a gentle lean forward onto your elbows in their direction.

This movement sends an unconscious message that you are confident in the answer. It is important not to step into the questioner's personal space as this may be perceived as overly assertive.

THANK THEM BECAUSE YOU ARE THE EXPERT

I am sure you have been in a situation where your inner voice's immediate response to a question is a resounding 'oh no' followed by a huge internal diatribe about why you wish you hadn't been asked that question. Of course this is hugely unhelpful when comes to responding and often shows on your face. With this in mind the third strategy for the world's leading expert process is to thank the questioner for the question. This applies no matter how tricky the question is or how negative the intent from the enquirer may be. It is even more powerful to accompany this with a gentle and genuine smile.

It is only right to thank them for the question when they have asked you about something you are a world's leading expert in. And you are, aren't you? Well if you follow this process then it suggests that you are. When we teach this to groups we encourage them to use those words exactly; however, when using the strategy in real life you will probably need to refine it slightly. Telling your finance director that you are the world's leading expert in budgeting may not be the best career move. Instead you might suggest it is an area you have been reviewing lately or that it is a subject you are passionate about. Of course if you are an expert I think it's perfectly acceptable to say so. Highly confident people aren't inappropriately humble.

SHARE THREE THINGS

There are many views on why the number three is such a significant number. Some attribute it to its implicit connection to the holy trinity. Others attach meaning to the long-held view that the brain was made up of three specific parts (a view now considered to be outdated). Whatever the reason, three is a powerful number and when establishing expertise it is the only number you need. From this moment on there are only three things that you need to know about anything.

When answering a question having smiled, taken a small step forward, thanked them for the question because this is an area you are an expert in, you now advise the questioner that there are three things they need to know. Underline this point by holding up three fingers.

It is now time to share your expertise. Answer the question with short, to-the-point answers. If you practise this process, don't prepare the answers in advance. The strategy enables you to tap into your expertise by getting you into a great state to answer the question, so notice how effectively you respond. In real situations you will have done your preparation; the strategy allows you to demonstrate your knowledge effectively.

As you make your three points, mark off your answers on each of the three fingers that you held up. This gives congruence to your answers and keeps you on track with your responses.

One last note, I always advise starting with three. If during the process you think the two points you have made are enough then after two you say, 'Actually I think they are the two most important things,' and stop. Similarly if you want to add one extra point, then do so, and then end but make sure you maintain eye contact and remain in the forward physiology.

Putting it all together

To help recap the process I will use an example from a new client meeting I had recently.

Client: Richard, can you tell us the most important things this senior team need to keep in mind to make this project a success?

Me: [*Keeping eye contact with the person posing the question and taking a small step forward*]. It's great that you've asked that as supporting senior teams is a specialism of mine. There are three things that make the biggest difference [*holding three fingers up*]. First is how well the business projects are connected to the strategy [*tapping one of the held-up* *fingers*]. Two is to support the groups to stay connected between sessions [*tapping the second finger*]. Third and most importantly is to ensure that of every member of the senior team models the new behaviours in every decision.

These replies led to another really positive conversation about how we support that client. It wasn't a question I was well prepared for, but the process helped me to access the knowledge that I had on the subject.

The examples I have given throughout the chapter have been work related, but the same strategy can be used no matter what environment the tricky question is posed in. From dealing with tough teenage questions to difficult doorstep conversations with neighbours, the world's leading expert process allows you to access your most resourceful self.

32 Confidence in confrontation

> *Only be you strong, and very courageous, then you will make your way prosperous, and then you will have good success.*
> Joshua 1:7

> *The brave man is not he who does not feel afraid, but he who conquers that fear.* Nelson Mandela

> *What separates the winners from the losers is how a person reacts to each new twist of fate.* Donald Trump

> *In the age-old contest between popularity and principle, only those willing to lose for their convictions are deserving of posterity's approval.* Gerald R. Ford

> *Never let the fear of striking out get in your way.* Babe Ruth

Can you define what conflict is for you? It is an interesting and important starting point for developing your confidence in times of conflict. People have very different conflict barometers. For some it is a cross word or raised voice at the family dinner table, while for others a full-volume shouting match across a boardroom is considered clearing the air and still doesn't qualify as real conflict. The importance of checking and potentially adjusting your conflict barometer stretches further than having your own internal strategies for being at your best in those moments of disagreements.

It is also crucial to develop your awareness of others' comfort with conflict. If you are uncomfortable with conflict it is likely that you will encounter robust conversations that only you see as conflict. An ex-colleague of mine used to ring me regularly after team meetings to check if he had been involved in any discussions that I considered conflict. The answer was almost always yes, but his comfort with and confidence during conflict was such that interactions had to be long, loud and highly emotive before he even considered there to be conflict. Until then they were just robust conversations.

Beyond this the confidence required for conflict is a calm one. Even if the moment calls for a raised voice or energetic response, your internal state must be composed. This steady state will help you to think clearly and keep the strategies in this chapter at your fingertips. You will be able to choose to embrace the conflict or walk away from it when the moment is right. Good conflict should result in a change for the better. This may be a different decision, or a change in relationship, or the commitment to a new course of action.

Conflict for conflict's sake is rarely healthy. Whether in work, home life or in other relationships, only engage in conflict where it is possible to have a healthy outcome, even if it doesn't feel good at that moment.

MAKE CONFRONTATION YOUR CHOICE

There are two main reasons that people don't walk away from conflict. The first is that they view walking away from a confrontation or challenge as weak. The second is simply that when you get embroiled in a conflict it is easy to forget that you can choose to remove yourself at any time.

It can take more strength to walk away, especially in arguments or conflicts that you have an emotional stake in or when you are being unfairly attacked, but it is important to recognize that you have options which maintain your integrity and show your strength rather than weakness.

The useful question to ask is, 'Why should I stay involved in this conflict?' Identifying the purpose of the conflict is a pivotal point in building your conflict confidence. For example, if you are in a project meeting at work and a peer is shouting down your ideas and being unfairly critical of your work, before responding ask yourself the question. If the answer is to protect your reputation and that of the team, then respond appropriately. If, however, the drive to respond is just to show the others in the meeting that your confronter is an idiot, then a neutral response such as, 'Of course I believe you are wrong, but I don't intend to get into this now,' is likely to be a more powerful one. If they continue with their attack they are just demonstrating that they are being driven by an unhelpful ego.

ADOPT A WINNING PHYSIOLOGY

The physiology that you adopt during a conflict will send the quickest message to those confronting you about your power and confidence in the situation. It will help to reduce the fight or flight mechanism that is triggered when you feel attacked and will help you to think more clearly. Here are three sub-strategies to maintain the right body posture:

Breathing

Keep your breathing slow and deep. Make sure that you are breathing from deep down in your stomach. The natural reaction to conflict is for our breathing to quicken and become shallower and you must counteract this.

Slowing your breathing down will help you to think clearly and maintain a sense of calm. Inhaling for a count of eight then exhaling for eight can be really useful in levelling your breathing.

Eye contact

Keep your eye contact steady and relaxed. Make sure the muscles around your eyes don't tense up. Avoid staring. The eye contact triangle formed by the other person's eyes and mouth is a great place to look. If you want to look away for a moment then look above or to the side of the person you are confronting. Avoid looking down. Finally don't blink too much. We tend to blink more under stress and this will send an unconscious message that you are feeling the pressure.

Stay centred

Those uncomfortable with conflict or confrontation will be familiar with a slightly dizzy or lightheaded feeling that grows as the tension does. It can feel literally like you are going to lose your balance. In moments of confrontation focus your internal attention on your abdomen. Imagine a heavy weight in the centre of your body which is keeping you steady. It can also be useful to focus for a moment on the feeling of your feet on the floor. These simple ways to keep yourself centred will again help you steady your sense of calm and control even in the most heated disagreements.

SAY LESS

At the exact time you want to rant and hit out verbally it is a great idea to say very little. If you have employed the other strategies in this chapter so far this will be easier. Keep your sentences short and to the point. For example, 'I don't agree' or, 'That isn't true' said firmly doesn't need any qualification.

Always stick to the facts. Your influence is reduced the moment you introduce speculation or assumption into your argument. Don't get derailed if your confronter is bringing up historical issues.

You must avoid insults, even if others are throwing them; they will only inflame the situation. There is nothing more unsettling than being smiled at by someone you are insulting. If those who you are in conflict with are swearing then it can be useful to mirror their language to demonstrate how they sound, but don't go on foul-mouthed rants. In most cases excessive use of bad language will damage your credibility.

All in all the less you are saying the more time and attention you have to listen for the holes in your confronter's case and to formulate the appropriate responses.

Putting it all together

I once encountered an expert on dealing with conflict who suggested we should approach it in the same way that Homer Simpson approaches doughnuts (mmmmm conflict). In theory I agree, but for many of us there is some significant groundwork to be done before we get to that point.

It is fair to say that those who are highly confident around conflict and confrontation embrace it and see the friction involved as energy for getting things done. They also know exactly the right time to walk away from unhealthy and unhelpful confrontation. I have spent a large part of my life avoiding any sort of confrontation at work and home and only recently realized how detrimental this is to getting the best results. I am not advocating seeking out conflict, but if it appears, and there is value in observing or being involved in it, then approach it with calm confidence.

In businesses today there is a growing desire to encourage staff to have courageous or difficult conversations. In the UK I think this is a tremendously healthy step. We have to move on from the culture that results in meetings which produce apparent agreement followed by bitching and sabotage.

In families confrontation will happen. When it does it should be dealt with and moved on from – genuinely – as quickly as possible. Many of the biggest family rifts come from issues that have been allowed to fester.

33) Building a confident team

❝ *There is no 'i' in team but there is in win.* Michael Jordan

❝ *The bottom line is, when people are crystal clear about the most important priorities of the organization and team they work with and prioritize their work around those top priorities, not only are they many times more productive, they discover they have the time they need to have a whole life.* Stephen Covey

❝ *Never doubt that a small group of thoughtful, committed people can change the world. Indeed. It is the only thing that ever has.* Margaret Mead

❝ *It is amazing how much people get done if they do not worry about who gets the credit.* Swahili proverb

❝ *Coming together is a beginning.*
Keeping together is progress.
Working together is success. Henry Ford

Organizations rely on teams for their success. In sport the stronger team will consistently outperform the group of talented individuals. Even in battle a fighting unit will only achieve its ultimate purpose when functioning as a highly effective team that has confidence in the abilities of the individuals within it.

If you are charged with creating a confident and successful team, the first place to start is defining what a team is.

The most useful definition of a team I have come across is the following:

'A group of people with a full set of complementary skills required to complete a task, job, or project.

Team members operate with a high degree of interdependence, share authority and responsibility for self-management, are accountable for the collective performance, and work toward a common goal and shared rewards(s). A team becomes more than just a collection of people when a strong sense of mutual commitment creates synergy, thus generating performance greater than the sum of the performance of its individual members.'

www.businessdictionary.com

This highlights the fact that, in order to be a team, there must be shared goals and rewards. The success of each team member must be reliant to some degree on others and the end result of the team's work together must be greater than would be achieved without that reliance and support.

If any of those elements aren't present, then you may be trying to create a team where one isn't required. For example a group of marketing managers with responsibility for their own business areas or brands may benefit from working together as a group to share ideas but it is unlikely that their success is reliant on the success of their colleagues. They are a workgroup not a team.

It is an important starting point. We often encounter managers whose confidence is being affected by their inability to get a work group to function as a team. Teams by this definition are desirable and effective but not mandatory. Before moving on to the strategies to create a confident team, ensure that the group you are focusing on are and should be a team.

DEVELOP A SHARED PURPOSE AND VISION

The form of shared goals that your team has will have a significant bearing on the sense of confidence and energy the team has. Strategic objectives are important in a business sense but they rarely engage and energize.

The importance of personal clarity of purpose has been highlighted in other parts of this book. Clarity of purpose for a team is equally important. A team that is absolutely clear on core purpose has the foundations for great decision-making and action.

The key question to ask is, 'Why does this team exist and why should anyone care?' Avoid answering the question as if it is a 'what' question. You and your team will know what you do; this question helps to clarify the purpose of having the team or business function in the first place. Get your team clear on purpose first and confidence will naturally increase.

While purpose is why you exist, vision is where you are going. Here is a simple vision question. 'If your team was hugely successful in the next 18 months, how would you and all of your stakeholders know?'

This question should be answered as richly as possible. Too much focus is often placed on the crafting of words that will look good to those outside of the team. A team's vision acts as a guide to give them clarity and energy for their work.

CREATE A POSITIVE TEAM CULTURE

Your team's culture will determine what is acceptable or unacceptable, important or unimportant, right or wrong, workable or unworkable. The culture of a team provides the sense of how we are with each other and how we do things around here.

Your choice as a manager or leader of a team is not whether it has a culture but what form it takes. Your team's culture will be defined by what you demonstrate through your behaviours and by what behaviours you reward and discourage within the This tacit culture building will always be more powerful than any stated cultural preferences if they are in conflict.

Announcing that you want an open and honest culture will be worthless if you make decisions behind closed doors and only share information on a need-to-know basis. Similarly the desire to have an innovative culture will always be killed if you allow team members to ridicule others' off-the-wall ideas.

First clearly define the culture that you want to foster in the team then describe specifically the acceptable and unacceptable behaviours that will nurture that culture. Be ready to lead the way to give others the confidence to co-create the culture.

ALLOW YOUR TEAM FREEDOM TO SUCCEED

How clear are your team on what success looks like? How well do their individual objectives help them to understand what a good job looks like and what a great job looks like? This is the first step in building a team's confidence in their ability to succeed. It is easy to overlook such a fundamental step but I have extensive experience in organizations where whole middle-management communities work on the basis that if they aren't getting their butts kicked by their boss they must be doing OK.

You also must be willing to step back and give your people the opportunity to flourish. Delegation is a challenge for so many managers and the confidence of their team suffers as a result. Make a clear distinction between the delegation of the what (task) and the how (approach). You are only truly delegating when you allow the individuals in the team to find their own approaches to the task. Even if they don't do it exactly as you would this doesn't necessarily make it wrong. You have to trust and support them to find their own way.

Few things will damage the confidence of a team quicker than an over-zealous superior who steps in at the first sign that members are finding their own way to achieve the task. Providing your team is operating with the purpose in mind, they are in service of the vision and, of course, within budget and the law, then be confident enough to let them flourish.

Putting it all together

If you are in the privileged position to lead or manage people in any walk of life it is a great opportunity to share the confidence that you have developed. Having clarified first if you are leading a team or a work group you must set about putting the structures in place that give the best opportunity for the team to flourish and succeed.

Even if the organization that you are part of doesn't promote the development of a core purpose and vision, take the initiative to create them for your team. When you do you will notice the development of very natural confidence within the team. Defining and most importantly demonstrating the culture that you want the team to adopt gives those team members who haven't yet discovered the secret of confidence the courage to make their mark. If you have team members who aren't willing to commit to the culture then you must tackle them appropriately.

Confidence within a team will always support its success. Technical ability and hard work have their place, but without a sense of confidence they will remain short term. Leadership sometimes requires you to do something different. Draw on everything that you have already learned and have the confidence to make a difference to the people work with and for you.

34 Building a confident organization

Vision is the art of seeing the invisible. Jonathan Swift

The best vision is insight. Malcolm Forbes

Dreams can become a reality when we possess a vision that is characterized by the willingness to work hard, a desire for excellence, and a belief in our right and our responsibility to be equal members of society. Janet Jackson

I've learned some exciting things – mostly, that people really want to help each other; and that, if you can lay out a vision for them – and that vision is sincere and genuine – they'll get interested. Michael J. Fox

Talent is the No. 1 priority for a CEO. You think it's about vision and strategy, but you have to get the right people first. Andrea Jung

What is an organization? Organizations get blamed for some of the world's biggest environmental challenges and are credited with some of the greatest achievements. But organizations don't really exist. It is a generalized term for a group of people with a particular purpose. In business sense this will be to provide a product or service and as a result create profit. It is easy to forget that the achievement of the purpose, vision and financial results of any business relies on its people. So when creating a confident organization the leader's focus must be largely people-focused.

Alexis Bowman is a Managing Director at BT Openworld and reflects this brilliantly through her thoughts on building a confident organization:

> When considering building a confident organization a leader must start with some fundamental questions. Does it exist now or are we all striving to create it? Is it a tangible state we can achieve? What is your definition of a 'confident organization'? As leaders, followers and observers do we know how to take our organizations to the next level? We will all have very different ways of viewing and answering some of these questions but it is my belief that wherever you start on that journey and whatever your vision for a 'confident organization' is, there are three fundamental strategies that will assist us all in our own very unique, challenging, yet exciting journey, be that in business, at home or in life generally.
>
> For me, a confident organization is one that can demonstrate a resistance and ability to adapt to volatility, to capitalize on challenges by making them our future opportunity to grow. It has a robust and positive attitude towards risk and ultimately will attract and retain talent. Confidence isn't just about being aggressive in its approach and strategy but it is about having an air of maturity that allows it to take positive challenges in a variety of environments, drives empowerment of its people in order to develop and grow the business. By nature confident organizations are not arrogant. They avoid narcissism and complacency and are clear they must take their stakeholders with them on their corporate journey.

EMPOWER AND GIVE OWNERSHIP

We talk about empowerment a lot in business, but the benefits of achieving real empowerment across an organization has no bounds. The approach to empowering the people in an organization to make decisions and become accountable for their own actions and outputs is critical. Getting the balance between empowering individuals within an organization and achieving hard business results is key.

To really empower individuals I believe we need to take the bold step away from purely driving our discussions via data and performance metrics. Yes we still need to keep an eye on the numbers and use them to complement our decision-making, but restricting decisions and activity to how we interpret results stifles the human view of what may really be happening and where new opportunities may exist.

We can help people to own their performance by shifting away from the classic top-down approach to management. Enabling an individual within their own local team and away from the classic top-down approach means we are not restricting their actions within the bounds of a data set or trying to force them to make decisions that are derived from someone else's view of the world. In doing this they will feel like they own part of the organization. Coming from a data-driven world, has been quite a big bit of learning for me and a shift in mindset!

The world shouldn't and doesn't revolve around numbers on a spreadsheet and equally I don't believe one size always fits all in approach, so empowering individuals within an organization to think and to be responsible for their own actions breeds creativity, loyalty and ultimately a greater ability to deliver. As individuals, when we feel like we are not only accountable for something but we also own our own destiny, then we really start to excel.

An organization that works as one team, promoting ownership and empowerment will be a more confident and robust organization. Removing the age-old dichotomy between being accountable but not having the power to own and make decisions yourself will lead you to a more confident organization. In my experience rewarding our best people with increased autonomy has been highly successful for both the individual and for the organization.

INVEST IN TALENT

We all accept that people are the foundation of nearly everything we do. People make the world go round! Investing in people and nurturing talent is an absolute must in creating a confident organization. In doing this you create an organization that isn't reliant on any one individual to make it succeed. Considering that almost all business transactions, business change, business growth and development require human interaction there should be no hesitation to invest in and develop the people who will be leading the business now and in the future. Organizations rely on people to change behaviours and create cultures. People are asked to be engaged and deliver outstanding results consistently. This is more than a work-for-money transaction and therefore it is an absolute necessity that you continue to invest in your people.

Look beyond the traditional approach to developing high fliers. Take time to review the strengths across the organization. While developing those people with the drive, passion and integrity to lead your organization is key, if you have individuals who aren't performing ask yourself why before moving them on. Is it just that you have a square peg in a round hole? By investing in them and helping them move into a role that they will excel at may benefit everyone. Don't be bound by a high level view of the world; there are gems to be found in some of the most unexpected places!

Remember too that when it comes to recruiting and forming teams, aim to achieve a balance between the technical capability needed and those who inspire and demonstrate real passion to achieve. Look for the skills that are difficult to train. Some people have a natural talent and can learn the technical aspects of a role but it is very difficult to do it the other way around. Once you have that team, continue to invest in and challenge them to become the best they possibly can. A confident work force breeds a confident organization.

KEEP AN EYE ON THE LONG GAME AND BE PREPARED

How often do you get to the end of the day having worked non-stop, had no lunch breaks and there are still a million emails sitting in your inbox? We tend as a working community to spend the majority of our time firefighting and reacting to the day's biggest story, but we very rarely schedule in that critical pro-active time. We sometimes are so engrossed in the now that tomorrow seems so very far away. If we as leaders model this way of working then naturally it will become the culture.

To become a confident organization you must create a balance between the long and short term. We need to move ourselves away from short-termism and prepare ourselves for what comes next. Where do we want to go? What is the long-term goal? How do we move away from fixing the symptoms of a problem to actually fixing the root cause and developing those blue sky ideas we all have? I believe there is one simple and effective strategy to doing this — create some space to breathe and think.

It sounds too simple to even mention, but the value your organization gains from allowing people time to think and prepare for tomorrow is huge. Giving people the time to think doesn't mean they will have all of the answers but it does mean they will develop a resilience and confidence in their ability to adapt and excel beyond today's view of the world. This in turn will create a more future-proofed and confident organization.

Putting it all together

Alexis Bowman's view of what is required to build a confident organization mirrors that of other forward-thinking business leaders. From LinkedIn's Jeff Weiner to Cougar Automation's Clive Hutchinson, senior people in organizations of all sizes are creating organizational cultures that engender trust and confidence. In a world where the pace of change continues to increase and what was once considered discontinuous change has now become continuous, this is crucial. Organizations in the 21st century are flexible and responsive. They must quickly reshape and refocus as market forces change while continuing to act in service of their core purpose. In order to do this effectively we have to create organizations, and by that I mean the people who are the organizations, that are confident enough to be creative, resilient and solve problems as they occur for the very first time.

(35) The confident job candidate

Choose a job you love, and you will never have to work a day in your life. Confucius

Pleasure in the job puts perfection in the work. Aristotle

Opportunities don't often come along. So, when they do, you have to grab them. Audrey Hepburn

Never put off till tomorrow what you can do today.
Thomas Jefferson

Success doesn't come to you, you go to it. Marva Collins

Being a participant in any recruitment process is a hugely challenging and stressful situation for most people. Not only do you need to be at your confident best but you have to showcase the skills and experience that you have in a way that your perspective hirer appreciates.

Applying the strategies in Chapter 23 (on using the power pose) will give you a huge advantage. It is the perfect preparation for any job interview. But the selection process starts way before then and as part of my research for this book I interviewed a number of people who are highly confident and successful in these processes. The good news is that there are some patterns which are easier to understand and apply.

Before we get to the strategies specific to getting hired, it is worth observing that each person I interviewed had a medium to high degree of day-to-day confidence. This doesn't mean that you can't get hired if you don't access your confidence in every area of your life. It simply means that you need to apply a range of strategies at the same time. Applying for jobs when your self-esteem is low in all areas of your life can mean failure is a self-fulfilling prophecy. As in any relationship you must value yourself before someone else can truly value you.

There is also the question of being clear on what the right role for you really is. Too many people apply for a job because they think it is right for them rather than being clear on what they really want or what their skills give them the best chance of being hired for. If you aren't currently employed, I appreciate that your net has to be cast wider, but that doesn't mean you should limit your job searches to the most obvious places. Value your skills and experience and ask yourself, 'What role would enable me to best demonstrate these skills?'

On these foundations you can apply the strategies that I have found to be most common in those highly confident in recruitment processes.

FOCUS ON YOUR ACHIEVEMENTS

Take a look at your CV. What does it suggest is most important about you? Your job history? Your address? Your qualifications? Now consider what your prospective employer would most value in their new recruit? I would suggest it is the ability to get the job done.

Restructure your CV and make your achievements its focus. In any previous job, what results did you achieve or what difference did you make? If your previous work experience is limited, focus on your achievements in other areas such as hobbies and interests or voluntary activities. One of the interviewees for this chapter shared that she is still asked more questions in interviews about her time as part of her school council than about her higher education, despite being in her 30s.

Carry this achievement focus through to your interview preparation. As you prepare answers to potential questions ensure that your language highlights achievement rather than process.

For example:

In response to: 'Can you give me an example of when you have led a team well?'

Say: 'When I led the team that delivered the highest customer satisfaction scores over the last three years, I ensured that everyone was clear on the vision and what their roles were in achieving it ...'

Rather than: 'I led the customer service team for three years and ensured that everyone was clear on the vision and what their roles were in achieving it ...'

This is a simple change but a powerful one that will distinguish you from others.

WHAT MAKES YOU DIFFERENT?

Most of your preparation should be focused on matching your skills and experience to the role, exploring how your personal values overlap with the company values, and matching your experiences to the potential questions you may be asked in the interview.

However, the strategy that differentiates the highly confident during hiring processes is that they also focus on what makes them different.

They all ask themselves variations on the following questions:

- What unique blend of skills, abilities and experience do I have that no one else does?
- What do I bring to the role that no other candidate does?
- What could I help my boss/team/organization achieve that they haven't thought of yet?
- How can I contribute beyond the role that I am being recruited for?

One of my interviewees was the least formerly qualified and in one of the most junior roles, yet was absolutely clear what he could add to any role that others couldn't. This more than anything made him fearless in his approach to the selection process.

WHAT WOULD HAVE TO HAPPEN FOR YOU TO HIRE YOU?

Imagine that you were in charge of recruitment for the role that you are applying for. What would have to happen for you to hire you? Consider the question from every angle.

- What would your CV need to look like?
- How would you need to sound during any telephone interactions?
- How would you need to dress?
- What would your demeanour need to be during the interview (remember to power pose beforehand)?
- What else would convince you to hire you if you were in charge?

It is useful to remember that recruitment processes are incredibly costly. The average cost to replace someone who has left an organization is estimated to be somewhere between £5,000 and £28,000 depending on their level in the business. The longer the process takes the greater the cost. Employers want to hire someone but they need it to be the right person. Answering these questions goes further than good preparation. They send a message to your brain that you are important in the context of the process and that you should feel confident about it. This forms the beginning of another confident loop.

Putting it all together

There are few selection procedures where the end result is guaranteed to be a positive one; whether you are in a job and looking for the next step or aiming to get back into employment, a confident approach will help you illuminate your qualities as a candidate. Going through the motions isn't enough. Nor is approaching it as a process. From the recruiter's side and from your side it is an opportunity to showcase yourself and to make new connections.

Approach it with energy and confidence and you will make an impression. You will also start another confidence loop.

Triggering your confidence going into the process and giving your best throughout it will leave you feeling more confident even if you don't get the role. Approaching it half-heartedly or even with energy but without confidence will leave you feeling that you didn't do your best and make tapping into your confidence more of a challenge next time.

The strategies that the highly confident people I interviewed shared are not complicated and provide a clear path for preparing in the best way for your next job opportunity.

36 The confident executive (1)

> He who has never learned to obey cannot be a good commander. **Aristotle**

> The best executive is the one who has sense enough to pick good men to do what he wants done, and self-restraint enough to keep from meddling with them while they do it. **Theodore Roosevelt**

> My biggest motivation? Just to keep challenging myself. I see life almost like one long university education that I never had, every day I'm learning something new. **Richard Branson**

> Leadership and learning are indispensable to each other. **John F. Kennedy**

> Energy and persistence conquer all things. **Benjamin Franklin**

In business, the ability to be confident and to develop others' confidence in you is a premium quality. I would consider it a requirement of leadership. In fact if I look at the four characteristics that followers most desire from leaders (honesty, inspiration, being future-focused and competent), all require the leader to have a genuine confidence in themselves to do them well.

During the course of my work I am fortunate enough to coach, consult with and learn from some great role models in outstanding organizations. What continues to surprise me after over a decade in this field is the humility that the best have. It is easy to forget that even the most senior people in the largest organizations with the biggest budgets have to develop their confidence. They also have to make choices and face events without a feeling of confidence.

While all of the tips and techniques in this book have been modelled on the highly confident, it is hugely important to me to bring you thoughts and ideas directly from the minds of some of those people. I particularly want to allow talented people in business that I experience as leaders to share their thoughts with you unedited. I trust you will find them useful.

Within moments of meeting Martyn Beachamp, International Director from Tesco Bank, I knew he was comfortable in himself and his approach to business. As his strategies demonstrate, this hasn't happened by accident. Beauchamp grew up in the east-end of London and has built a career with some of the leading names in the financial services industry. He has worked around the world, is fluent in several languages and yet he still sees confidence as something to be nurtured. Here are his lessons from a confident leader.

PREPARE THE IMPORTANT THINGS

For me, confidence is a state – my state – and so I own it. Confidence can be acquired and cultivated but it has to be owned first. That my confidence is largely in my own hands has been one of the biggest and simplest revelations of my professional life. Knowing this helps me manage my mind-talk and frees me to focus on the strategy that matters most to my confidence levels: building resilience through continuous preparedness.

Being prepared gives me confidence. I don't think I'm particularly unusual in that sense. Many of us have agonized over the questions we might be asked on a particular line on any page in a hundred-slide presentation. But as I've progressed through my career, I've realized two things about preparing for confidence.

I find that I spend more and more of my preparation time on state management. For instance, I'll prepare carefully for a big presentation to cement my confidence, but I'll now spend as much time thinking about things like knowing my audience and their motives and coalitions, or how to stay composed if

I'm tripped by a low-ball question, as I will about the remotest possibility that I might be asked a detailed question on Appendix IX. In preparation, I'll prime myself with confidence by focusing on a moment when I was at my best and viewing it as a spectator. Knowing myself and then the facts – in that order – gives me the confidence I need to be effective in these set-piece events.

HAVE RESILIENT CONFIDENCE

In between these events are dozens of daily interactions in which the right level of confidence can make all the difference to my impact. It's impossible to prepare in the formal sense for these moments. Which brings me to the second thing I've realized about my confidence: it's the resilience of my confidence that matters – the ability to substitute wild swings with a more manageable ebb and flow within the tolerance limits required for me to lead with impact. I do this through a form of continuous preparation.

Here are some examples. I make sure I spend time each week preparing a range of short, punchy elevator speeches on the issues that matter most, just in case I bump into a key stakeholder. I stay alert, externally focused and keep my eyes open for new ideas. I read widely but economically, focusing on a manageable number of trusted sources, and usually at the same time most nights after I've put the kids to bed, so it's locked down into my routine. I study and know my stakeholders. I don't obsess over it, but I keep it simple and make it a process. I find it consistently improves my ability to prosper in conditions of ambiguity, which makes me feel confident and strengthens my impact.

BUILD CONFIDENCE IN DISCOMFORT

'I deliberately work on being confident when uncomfortable. I want to know that when I'm out of my comfort zone, I've got enough about me to draw on. I use preparedness to give me that confidence: throughout my career, I've consciously and consistently sought out opportunities to test myself outside of my comfort zone. And there are tactical measures I take: when I envisage being uncomfortable, I'll often wear a suit. I know it makes me feel more alert and energized. By owning and strategically managing my discomfort, I feel I can approach areas of difficulty or times of crisis with a greater degree of confidence.

I see confidence as a means to an end: I want to be confident because when I am consistently confident, my personal impact is greater. By playing my preparedness long and making it a process, I feel best equipped to lead with confidence and, on those occasions when my confidence takes a knock, to quickly bounce back.

Putting it all together

Martyn Beauchamp's confidence shows a level of thinking that moves beyond the day-to-day practices involved in the development of self-confidence. He outlines the basis of a more strategic and politically savvy approach to maintaining and developing the level of confidence required to deliver in a challenging role in a dynamic organization. The greatest lesson from Martyn's story is to see the preparation of your confidence as at least as important as your preparation of facts, figures and information. His confidence is deep and genuine but it is also nurtured and developed.

Martyn is unusual only in the detailed nature of his preparation. He is not unique in the sense that what he does can be replicated by anyone who is willing to pay attention to the things that they do. In my work with him, I consider him to be one of the most politically astute leaders I have encountered. I believe that much of the skill he operates with comes from the same principles that he shares in this chapter. If you adopt this strategy, I believe the approach will allow the natural talent you have to flourish and to allow others around you to recognize it.

37 The confident executive (2)

   ❝ *Strength does not come from winning. Your struggles develop your strengths. When you go through hardships and decide not to surrender, that is strength.* Arnold Schwarzenegger

   ❝ *Spending too much time focused on others' strengths leaves us feeling weak. Focusing on our own strengths is what, in fact, makes us strong.* Simon Sinek

   ❝ *Many of us feel stress and get overwhelmed not because we're taking on too much, but because we're taking on too little of what really strengthens us.* Marcus Buckingham

   ❝ *Decision is a sharp knife that cuts clean and straight; indecision, a dull one that hacks and tears and leaves ragged edges behind it.* Gordon Graham

   ❝ *In time of difficulties, we must not lose sight of our achievements.* Mao Tse-tung

My interview with Ray Biggs, the Head of Customer Contact at Sainsbury's, brought back into focus the importance of focusing on what you are already good at. Since reading Marcus Buckingham's *Now Discover Your Strengths* I have been an advocate of developing the positive skills and attributes that you have rather than just focusing on the things you aren't yet good at. According to Buckingham's website (www.tmbc.com/), if you find someone who can answer 'yes' to the question, 'At work do you have the opportunity to do what you do best every day?' you will find a business unit with higher productivity, higher customer satisfaction and higher employee retention.

Buckingham argues that we must change the culture of recruiting people, focusing their training and development on their weaknesses. This is a great opportunity to ask yourself, 'Am I building a career that plays to my strengths?' You can expand the question beyond your work: 'Are the things that I spend most time on allowing me to draw on my most positive attributes?'

Ray's approach to leadership and the development of his confidence as a senior leader in the organization may not have been formulaic, but the following are his clear strategies that can be replicated if you want to build your confidence as a leader in your organization.

USE YOUR STRENGTHS AS YOUR FOUNDATION

'Most people don't know that I have a background in drama. I actually have a degree in it and drama is all about communication. It is no surprise then that my style is hugely people-focused. Confidence in communication at a senior level is self-fulfilling. The more you communicate the more confident you become in it. The more confident you are the more you do it.

The very best development I have had in my career helped me to understand why I do what I do and how those things are successful for me. For example, I am not naturally a structured person. The realization that I could still be successful was a real lightbulb moment for me. I need to build my team with this in mind, but I have enough confidence in my thought process that if am presented with a problem I let my unconscious work on it and the answer will pop out.

Self-awareness is crucial. Reflect on success experiences from the past and identify what has helped you to achieve what you have. Know what you're good at; recognize what you're not good at. I really believe there is a much greater benefit in developing your strengths rather than marginally improving the things you aren't so good at. If you look at yourself honestly you can create a career path that allows you to move up the direction of your strengths not your weaknesses.'

BUILD YOUR NETWORK

'Leadership is interesting for me. The frustration I have is that you can't prescribe leadership. It is what you do moment by moment. I don't think leaders' reputations or confidence are really built at the big events. It is during the conversations at the coffee machine. It is how you make eye contact with people as you pass them in the corridor and whether you say good morning to them no matter how busy your mind is.

Leadership is about being able to get things done and that relies on building relationships which in turn relies on your ability to communicate. As I have said before, communication is self-fulfilling. It relies on self-belief and self-awareness and it builds self-belief and self-awareness.

I believe that when people struggle in a management role it isn't usually the role, it is their relationships or lack of them in the organization that they are struggling with. During my time with Argos I led through the network that I had developed over the course of eight years in the business. When I joined Sainsbury's I was aware that it was such a huge organization I had to trade on my confidence to build a network. Until I had a strong network I wasn't completely effective. The primary goal was to build the network so I could get up to speed as quickly as possible. If I hadn't spent time in the past reflecting on my successes and strengths this process would have been so much more difficult. It also requires an element of hard work. I have a belief that if I work hard I will get on. As I first stepped into that new role I knew the effort that I made would help me through. I knew that I was unlikely to feel completely ready for the new role, but that feeling unsure was OK as long as the network was growing.'

TAKE CALCULATED CHANCES

'When I was a little younger I used to go for jobs that I thought were too big for me. I would often get to interview stage and that was a boost. This is an example of taking a calculated chance. People with more experience than me wouldn't even apply in case they didn't get it. They would be left wondering 'what if?' I would be left with more experience and more confidence. You have to be prepared to take risks and see disappointments for what they are — just disappointments.

If something isn't working stop doing it and do something different instead. When this feels like a risk or that it will be difficult I just ask myself, how hard can this be? If your gut says you can do it then make the change. I don't believe that there is anyone whose gut feeling is wrong more than it's right and my career turned when I began to trust my gut feeling more. It was noticeable that other people began to trust me when I trusted myself more.

Taking calculated chances also means having the confidence to stand up and be counted. Being able to say, 'Sorry, I really don't understand' or, 'No, this is wrong' in a skilled enough way is crucial. If you haven't got the skill to do that yet, then you must develop it. If you don't have a voice that impacts on your confidence much more than having a voice and not being listened to. Have the right conviction and stand up to be counted on the right thing.

While you have to accept that not every decision you make will be right, by being willing to make considered leaps of faith people will think you are the expert. When people tell you you are an expert it helps to bolster your confidence. As your confidence gets stronger you will be more willing to take a leap of faith. It is a great sequence to begin.'

Putting it all together

The strategies that have served Ray so well over almost two decades in the retail sector should give great hope to any aspiring young leader in business today. Nothing that has helped him to a senior role in one of the biggest brands in the UK is impossible to replicate. His confidence in his communication and decision-making comes essentially from taking action, reviewing his successes and doing more of what works.

38 The confident entrepreneur

> **It's fine to celebrate success but it is more important to heed the lessons of failure.** Bill Gates

> **I don't know the key to success, but the key to failure is trying to please everybody.** Bill Cosby

> **Your time is limited, so don't waste it living someone else's life. Don't be trapped by dogma – which is living with the results of other people's thinking. Don't let the noise of others' opinions drown out your own inner voice. And most important, have the courage to follow your heart and intuition. They somehow already know what you truly want to become. Everything else is secondary.** Steve Jobs

> **Every time you state what you want or believe, you're the first to hear it. It's a message to both you and others about what you think is possible. Don't put a ceiling on yourself.** Oprah Winfrey

> **It takes 20 years to build a reputation and five minutes to ruin it. If you think about that, you'll do things differently.** Warren Buffett

I can speak with first-hand experience that being an entrepreneur is both hugely rewarding and hugely challenging. Being your own boss is a privilege balanced by the occasional sense that you are at the beck and call of your clients. Creating, maintaining and growing a business has been one of the toughest things I have done in my life, yet I wouldn't change it for the world.

In the recent economic downturn a record number of businesses were created in the UK. This means a record number of entrepreneurs whose core confidence will undoubtedly be tested to its extreme. Around 50 per cent of businesses fail in the first three years and with the houses, family incomes and self-esteem of the entrepreneurs creating these business on the line, it is important to take every opportunity to make confident decisions that work out for the best.

As this chapter implies, I believe that anyone creating a new business must look beyond the immediate challenge of creating one that is financially viable. In order to be a confident and happy business owner you must aim to create an operation that moves you towards the life you want to lead. It is so important to me. I have met too many talented people who have focused too highly on the lifestyle element of the business and ended up with an enterprise where profits were so low they had to work every hour just to keep it solvent. Equally I have met many people who have created hugely profitable businesses that kept them away from their families and allowed them precious little time to enjoy the fruits of their labour.

This chapter doesn't profess to give the answer to every question an entrepreneur will face, but it does present three strategies that I have observed the most genuinely confident business owners use and what they focus on consistently.

IDENTIFY YOUR NICHE

To get straight to the heart of the matter, too many businesses are created to provide too much to too many people. This is driven by the fear of the business owner that they may miss out on a sector of the market.

In almost every business sector you won't create a highly profitable business without identifying a niche. If you are creating a new business it can feel counter-intuitive to exclude some of your market. The reality is that people pay more for expertise or difference so you can make more money for less work or risk.

For example if the roof on your house needed to be repaired and you saw the following two vans on your way to work, which of the following would you choose to call?

- The generic white van. A little rusty around the edges with 'Joe Bloggs Repairs – no job too big or too small. Call us now for reliable work for a cheap price'.
- The silver Mercedes van. Clean and well driven with 'Joe Bloggs Specialist Roof Repairs – high quality work from the roofing specialists'.

Around 90 per cent of people will go for the latter despite the expectation that they will pay more than if they contacted the first company. The 10 per cent generally do so because they haven't got the money for the latter company and feel that they have to make do for now.

Which do you want to be in your business sector? How do you want to make money (remembering that turnover is vanity and profit is sanity)?

Ask yourself the following questions to begin the process of identifying your niche:

- What makes my product or service different from the rest?
- Who would I love to do business with (and do they have the right budget to do so)?
- What would I have to change to double my profits with the same turnover?
- How can I position myself differently from the rest of the market?
- What would be so enjoyable that I couldn't help but make a ton of money while still benefiting others?

BE CLEAR ON WHAT YOU DON'T DO

To support the identification of your niche you must get clear on what you don't do and who you don't do business with. This requires real confidence but, as you reap the rewards, it will reinforce your confidence in your decision-making processes. You must be ruthless in your thinking. For example, I coached a former senior Head of Learning and Development who had decided to set up her own development business. When I raised the question of niche, she told me she had considered that already and was going to focus on management, leadership and coaching for middle and senior managers. It took some convincing her that this wasn't a niche as it was including way too many people. This kind of approach will lead you to be seen as a generalist and therefore not allow you to command the fees that a specialist does.

In the retail world, in recent times, those at the very end and very bottom end of the market have thrived. Those who target everyone as their customers have faced the biggest challenges.

Answer the following questions:

- What products or services do I absolutely not provide?
- What kind of customers don't I want to do business with?
- What sectors do I want to avoid?
- Who shouldn't be able to afford what I offer?

BE BRILLIANT AT BALANCE

I once attended a seminar during which the expert speaker on the stage told a rapt audience that in order to become a millionaire entrepreneur you must be willing to sacrifice everything. He shared stories about missing out on time with his family, missing holidays and obsessively working through the night. I decided at that moment that if that was what it took to become a millionaire then I would rather continue with my very happy and comfortable lifestyle. In fact I know that is not what is required. I know many millionaire entrepreneurs who would credit their focus on balance as a key-contributing factor to their success. That is not to say they don't work incredibly hard but they don't do it at all costs.

Christine Riordan, the Provost and Professor of Management at the University of Kentucky, wrote a wonderful article on balance for the *Harvard Business Review* 'Work-life 'balance' isn't the point, 4 June 2013) and suggested three key strategies for finding your balance:

- Strive for worklife effectiveness, not balance.
- Define success in all categories of your life.
- Maintain control.

Integrate this approach into your initial business plan. If your business already exists, challenge your thinking about balance and how present you have to be for your business to be a success. Highly confident entrepreneurs know that they must take time to recharge their batteries to avoid burnout. Make this part of your business strategy.

Putting it all together

Entrepreneurs are likely to be the drivers of the new economy. As the numbers of self-employed and new business owners grows, so does the need for an understanding of the confidence challenges they face. If you are already in this position then you know first-hand what this means. Every day brings decisions that call for you to be brave and certain.

A keen understanding of the foundations of confidence and the applications of techniques throughout this book will help you to stay on course and make good decisions when all around you are falling into doubt and panic. The three strategies in this chapter will help you to lay the foundations of a business which has the opportunity to survive and thrive.

My wish for you is that you create more than a successful business. Frankly, life is too short to just create a successful business. My wish is that you use the opportunity to build the life you want to lead with your business as the fuel for doing so. Doing successful work that makes you come alive is a wonderful way to anchor confidence in your business life and beyond. If that work also makes a positive difference to others then your legacy becomes one that stretches far beyond the simple creation of a business.

(39) The confident introvert

❝ *I always try to be myself. Ever since I was an introverted kid, I'd get on stage and be able to break out of my shell.*
Beyoncé Knowles

❝ *I'm quite introverted but I'm not shy.* Marian Keyes

❝ *Where I feel the most productive and engaged is when I'm buried in code, buried in some project, tweaking some designs. I'm certainly introverted.* David Karp

❝ *The limited circle is pure.* Franz Kafka

❝ *Knowledge speaks but wisdom listens.* Jimi Hendrix

There is a common misconception that an introvert is a person who is shy. In fact being an introvert is quite a different thing. Shyness means feeling apprehension and nervousness around others. An introvert can be shy but many extroverts also feel the apprehension in others' company; they just react to it differently. Put simply, an introvert is someone who is energized by being alone and whose energy, particularly their mental energy, is drained by being around other people.

Introverts are more concerned with their inner world. They enjoy thinking and exploring their thoughts and feelings. They often avoid social situations because of the drain of being around people. This is true even if they have good social skills. After being with people for any length of time, such as at a party, they need time alone to 'recharge'.

When introverts want to be alone and are forced to be with others it can be particularly wearing. They simply want the time to be with their own thoughts and being with people, even people they like and are comfortable with, can prevent them from achieving their desire to be quietly introspective.

Introverts are often strong conversationalists; however those conversations are generally about ideas and concepts, not about what they consider the trivial matters of social small talk.

So why have a specific chapter on confidence for introverts? Well my guess is if you are asking that question you probably aren't introverted and there is great value in reading on to understand more. For those of you who have read this introduction so far and are saying, 'Yes, that is me', then you are likely to have faced the challenges that growing and showing your confidence as an introvert brings.

The myths about introverts are common and unfortunately widely believed, especially in many sections of the business world. You are likely to have been labelled as shy, not liking people, always wanting to be alone and not liking to be in crowds. None of which are true but how do you show your confidence to others when doing so for long periods drains your energy? Many of the introverts I work with feel that it is an extroverted world and to get on you have to somehow be 'fixed'. I hope that in time the power of introversion is more valued by the media and social commentators, but until then here are three simple strategies to help others see your power without your battery running out.

ENLIGHTEN THE EXTROVERTS

I had best come clean now. I am an extrovert. More importantly, my affection and value for introversion came relatively recently. I had been blindsided by the myths too. I thought I should just leave the introverts alone to be quiet together. Remember that introverts and extroverts perceive their worlds quite differently. While this may seem like an obvious statement it needs to be emphasized. It is more than a general difference of opinion. For many extroverts the idea that being alone recharges your mental energy is quite odd. They want to be with others to refresh theirs and make decisions on this basis. If you are working with a group of extroverts take time to explain your introversion to them. Don't wait until your energy is low to do it. Too often introverts are forced to explain why they want to be alone or why they are being quiet at exactly the wrong time. Remember, the extroverts assume there is something wrong with you and will try and be social to perk you up.

A little information is usually enough to stop the extroverts badgering you every time you want a moment with your thoughts, along the lines of, 'I'm a bit of an introvert, so when I have been in a meeting all day sometimes I just like to spend some time in my own company or I get a little quiet. It's nothing personal and there is nothing wrong, so don't worry if you notice me joining in the conversation a little less' As one extrovert put it, 'If we aren't talking often we aren't thinking. We forget that isn't true of introverts'.

Share your introversion confidently and you are likely to get huge support from fellow introverts in the group.

STAGGER YOUR RECHARGE TIME

This is by no means a time management book, but some extra thought to your planning can go a long way to keeping your introverted confidence up. One particular introvert I work with plans her diary around almost a monthly cycle. For three weeks she will attend meetings, then arrange social activities and even host parties at weekends. She then has a week where she works alone and avoids seeing anyone socially. The challenge for her is week three when her mental energy is so low she struggles to function at anywhere near her full capability. Even her social interactions are less enjoyable and have a forced sense to them.

It is much healthier for introverts to stagger their interactions. If you have a socially busy period at work, then reduce activities outside of work that impact on your energy. If it is possible to leave gaps between meetings then do so and ensure that time is used for activities that recharge.

Be discerning about who you spend time with both in work and beyond. Social circles change over time and as an introvert you can benefit from spending more time with people who demand less from you in social situations.

Overall, plan your time and interactions in such a way that you don't wait until your energy is gone completely before you have time on your own. Doing this will only reinforce the introvert stereotype.

HANG OUT IN BIGGER GROUPS

This may sound a little counter-intuitive at first, but spending time in larger groups can be less draining than in smaller ones. Smaller social groups can be more intense and require more interactions. In larger groups you are likely to be required to contribute to the conversation less and to be left to your thoughts more.

I recently ran a training event for 120 people in an organization where groups are usually limited to 12 participants. One introverted member of the group spoke to me during the lunch break to say that she was enjoying being able to learn without being constantly put on the spot. She could choose to contribute to the conversation when she felt it was valuable and not just for the sake of it.

If your job requires you to attend networking events, I would highly recommend groups attended by larger numbers of people. Smaller networking events with the traditional structured small talk are hugely draining for introverts. Larger events allow you to choose the conversations you get involved in.

Even public speaking can be more palatable when larger numbers are involved. One executive shared that she much preferred speaking to groups of 500 than to groups of 20, as she was more comfortable with the less personal nature of the sessions. She also said she much preferred being on the stage than having to make small talk with her colleagues afterwards.

What opportunities can you create to experiment with spending time in larger groups?

Putting it all together

If you are extroverted and have made it this far through the chapter, I applaud you. Your new insight will not only help the introverts you spend time with, it will also help you to influence more subtly with a wider range of people.

If you are an introvert, I know that there are times when it feels like the world is run by extroverts. From presidents to CEOs, the extroverts are cast as the great trailblazers, influencers and leaders. Be sure that isn't true. Remember, you only see the extroverted behaviours, you don't see the preparation and recovery that some of those in the public eye undertake to be able to perform in this way. Also, there is without doubt great power in introversion.

In her thought-provoking TED Talk, Susan Cain (author of *Quiet: The Power of Introverts in a World That Can't Stop Talking*) has three calls for action for the extroverted world:

'Number one: Stop the madness for constant group work. And I want to be clear about what I'm saying, because I deeply believe our offices should be encouraging casual, chatty cafe-style types of interactions you know, the kind where people come together and serendipitously have an exchange of ideas. That is great. It's great for introverts and it's great for extroverts. But we need much more privacy and much more freedom and much more autonomy at work. School, same thing. We need to be teaching kids to work together, for sure, but we also need to be teaching them how to work on their own. This is especially important for extroverted children too. They need to work on their own because that is where deep thought comes from in part.

Number two: Go to the wilderness. Be like Buddha, have your own revelations. I'm not saying that we all have to now go off and build our own cabins in the woods and never talk to each other again, but I am saying that we could all stand to get inside our own heads a little more often.

Number three: Take a good look at what's inside your own suitcase (her metaphor for what is really important to you) and why you put it there. So extroverts, maybe your suitcases are also full of books. Or maybe they're full of champagne glasses or skydiving equipment. Whatever it is, I hope you take these things out every chance you get and grace us with your energy and your joy. But introverts, you being you, you probably have the impulse to guard very carefully what's inside your own suitcase. And that's okay. But occasionally, just occasionally, I hope you will open up your suitcases for other people to see because the world needs you and it needs the things you carry.'

40 The confident influencer

> *It's easier to win when everyone wants you to win.* Randy Komisar

> *A life lived in fear is a life half-lived.* Spanish proverb

> *If you're going to perform inception, you need imagination. You need the simplest version of the idea – the one that will grow naturally in the subject's mind. Subtle art.* From the script of *Inception*

> *Whatever words we utter should be chosen with care for people will hear them and be influenced by them for good or ill.* Buddha

> *Wise men speak because they have something to say; Fools because they have to say something.* Plato

If you have ever wished that you had the confidence to ask for what you wanted, or if you have avoided a negotiation just in case you didn't get what you wanted, then this is the chapter for you.

Haider Imam is a gently challenging and playful former colleague of mine who also happens to be an expert in the field of influence. He is the author of *Straight To Yes* and is your coach for the next few pages.

… And in the blink of an eye, the dinosaurs were gone and a new world order emerged. 185 million years of rule by brute force and stealth disappeared overnight, paving the way for an increasingly gentle, diverse and interdependent ecosystem. I believe a similar transition is occurring in how we interact, influence and achieve success both at work and at home.

Okay, okay, maybe a little overdramatic but, as Bob Dylan said, the times they are a changin'. Thankfully for those of us with slightly quieter natures, having an impact is no longer about displaying the loudest voice, the biggest shoulder pads or the most creative skulduggery. We know now that these stereotypically 'Wall Street' behaviours are both unsustainable and dangerous to ourselves and the wider system.

So what is the new way? The latest scientific research presents us with some wonderful paradoxes in that, in the game of success, nice guys actually finish first. And last. That rejection is actually a key to success. And that our ideas are far more persuasive when people think they came up with those ideas themselves. So, here are three of my favourite lessons in influence that I am confident will serve you well.

FEED YOUR NETWORK AND DON'T OVEREAT

In today's interconnected, interdependent world, don't we need to look after one another more than ever to realize our ambitions? For many of us, however, our kind and generous behaviours have sometimes led to having figurative sand kicked in our faces, watching the wrong person get promoted or resolving, 'No more Mr Nice Guy!' The trouble is that wearing the mask of Ming the Merciless only lasts a few weeks before we revert to type because masks are notoriously uncomfortable and fiddly to keep in place. If only being a kind, decent person could equate with being a top performer in our field. Well, turns out it can.

Wharton Business School's top professor Adam Grant published a body of research in his 2013 book *Give and Take* outlining just that. In his work, he identified three kinds of behaviours or 'types': 'givers,' 'matchers' and 'takers.' Givers operate from generosity, doing favours for people in their network. Matchers operate from *quid pro quo* – keeping score of favours and demanding the same amount in return. Takers operate from self-interest, looking to see how much value they can extract from the system around them. Grant's research looked at how successful each type is in their organization or field and presented various conclusions:

1. Takers end up near the bottom of the success ladder: the lone wolf attitude of dog-eat-dog, withholding information and self-interest means that, over the long term, takers are despised by those around them, resulting in a fall from grace.
2. Matchers end up in the middle of the success ladder: they reap what they sow.
3. Givers end up at the bottom of the ladder: constantly responding to people's requests for help, empathizing and putting others' interests ahead of their own means they are least productive and successful.
4. Givers end up at the ... top of the ladder: wait ... what?

Fascinatingly, Grant's research showed that nice guys finish first ... and last. The difference? Quite simple, it seems. While both sets of givers generously feed their network of colleagues, friends, suppliers and even competitors by doing useful things for them, unsuccessful givers overEAT. That means they overindulge in (E) empathy, (A) availability and (T) timidity. Being emotionally over-involved in other people's stuff, giving so much time to others that our own work suffers and being too timid to ask for what we want or need (or ask for help) is a great recipe for last place. Top givers were empathetic enough, asked for what they needed and, while generous with their favours, protective of their time.

- Go through your contacts list or address book every few weeks to remind yourself who is actually in your network.
- Make strides to understand what people in your network want or need: what are their desires, hobbies, interests, challenges, anxieties or opportunities? What do the people who are important to them need?
- Regularly schedule these 'five-minute favours' for an hour or two in your diary each week and do them in one block, not *individually*.

COURT REJECTION

Many people spend their lives nervous of looking incompetent, pushy or greedy. I believe it mostly all comes back to a fear of being rejected. Since we're social creatures, being isolated is a death sentence: biological self-preservation encourages us to stay in good favour with people. We tend to ask for a lot less, a lot less often and with a lot less conviction, just in case we're rejected and fall from grace. And yet successful persuaders collect more rejections than most people because they ask for more, more often and with more conviction than most people.

So, here's a three-level exercise to build your rejection muscle and achieve oneness with being declined – and know that it is a muscle, that grows with practice. The aim is to intentionally seek out small rejections and when you get them, to realize that your internal health and wellbeing remains intact. Feel free to substitute the following examples for your own:

Beginner level: Next time you're eating somewhere that gives diners sachets of ketchup, mustard and mayonnaise, politely ask if you can have one extra sachet for free, regardless of how many you have on your table or plate.

Intermediate level: Next time you're in a restaurant, politely request something that's not written on their menu, simply because you're in the mood for it.

Master level: When you're next buying something in a shop, ask for a particular item for free.

Learn to love rejection because the more often you're being rejected, the more often you're asking; the more often you're asking, the more you'll start hearing 'yes'. And it's perhaps useful to remember that in life, if you ever happen to cross the line, it's generally easier to seek forgiveness than to ask permission!

PULL FIRST, PUSH LATER

Whenever we try to convince, persuade or push someone to accept our ideas, we can inadvertently create resistance and push-back (it's called psychological reactance – a natural defence mechanism). This is particularly the case with people over whom we have no direct authority. And teenagers.

So, rather than purely relying on pitching, suggesting, telling and 'Why-don't-you-ing' we can aim to 'pull', to let the other person have at least some input into the idea, so they feel that it is partly or wholly their own. Once they articulate the idea, they'll feel vastly more committed to following it through.

Here's how: avoid saying, 'Here's what I think we should do …' or 'Can I share my ideas about (…) with you and why I think it'll be great for us?' or anything that involves you 'selling' your ideas.

Instead, try sharing your desired outcome explicitly (for example, 'I'm really keen to head up a finance project team …' or 'I'd like to visit the Chicago office to forge links and share practices …') and then asking any of the following questions, or your own versions of them:

- 'What are your thoughts on how that might benefit us/ you/the department?'
- 'How could you see that working, practically?'
- 'What would have to happen for you to be happy to sign off on that?'
- 'How would you pitch that to your team?'

When you hear answers that support your outcome, express interest and probe more. If you hear a flat refusal, acknowledge their answer and firmly ask the question again, emphasizing words like 'could', 'might' and 'would' to make it safe and hypothetical.

Particularly when we have to influence upwards or persuade big egos, pulling on intrinsic motivations is always a better way to get what you want. And you can always 'pitch' afterwards if you need to.

Putting it all together

Notice how many of Haider's strategies feel comfortable and how many challenge your current influencing boundaries. During a team meeting Haider once challenged me to go to a shop and ask for something for free. I refused on the basis that it was wrong to ask for something for nothing. As the rest of the team returned from the experiment with some pretty cool things that they had picked up for nothing but a human exchange, I realized that I needed to expand my influencing bandwidth.

As your confidence becomes more grounded, challenge yourself to influence in new and more daring ways and enjoy the rewards. Here is a summary of Haider's strategies for influencing with confidence:

1. Your success potential is a function of your network strength.
2. To strengthen your network, proactively feed it, regularly and generously, but never overEAT.
3. Practise collecting rejections of increasing size.
4. Instead of pitching your ideas first, offer your outcome and ask the other person or group how that could be wonderful.

By marrying your goals with the goals of those you're hoping to influence, it's possible to transform both your results and your relationships.

41 The confident public speaker

> *To suppress free speech is a double wrong. It violates the rights of the hearer as well as those of the speaker.*
> Frederick Douglass

> *Try to be as good a listener as you are a speaker. Don't just put the emphasis on saying things. Listen.* Jennifer Lynch

> *Being a comfortable public speaker, which involves easily being able to go off-script, strongly signals competence.* Amy Cuddy

> *It's much easier to be convincing if you care about your topic. Figure out what's important to you about your message and speak from the heart.* Nicholas Boothman

> *Always give a speech that you would like to hear.* Andrii Sedniev

In October 2013 a poll found that more people feared public speaking more than they feared being buried alive. One hack suggested this was 'because being buried alive at least would be private. No audience to watch you writhe'. These findings aren't unique. A similar poll in the USA in the nineties put public speaking at the top of a list of things that those surveyed were afraid of. Number two on the list was death. The suggestion that some people would rather die than speak in public is of course ridiculous, but it shows the power of negative thinking that people have about presenting to audiences. Indeed even the most confident sports and business people I have worked with over the years have found this to be one of the biggest challenges. So in this chapter I would like to share with you some ways to tap into your natural charisma and present with confidence.

Before we get on the stage, it is well worth remembering the power of mental rehearsal as covered in other chapters. If the pictures and movies that you are playing in your head prior to the presentation are of it going badly you are increasing the likelihood of that happening and making yourself feel bad too. Create a rich mental picture of the whole presentation or speech going brilliantly and keep it in focus in the lead up to the event.

It is also worth remembering that most of your audience want you to do well. There are very few situations where those in attendance want you to fail. Stay positive in your thoughts about their thoughts as a way to boost your confidence and use these strategies to keep it high.

HONE YOUR GESTURES

In my earlier days working with large groups I studied some of the most charismatic and confident presenters, trainers and speakers in the world. My quest was to find out what helped them keep their audiences' attention so well. I was surprised to find that the single thing they all had in common was that their gestures were more pronounced than others who were less successful in front of large groups.

This doesn't mean that you have to make wild and extravagant gestures, but when you do, make the movement more pronounced. For example, if you point to something on a visual aid then do so with a quick, definite movement.

To give you more of an idea, place the palms of your hands together then move them out to around a shoulder-width apart slowly and with your hands relaxed. Now place them back together and do the same again but moving your hands quickly and while keeping them tensed. Imagine you were using these gestures while describing the projected growth of your company. Which would be more powerful? Remember it isn't always about making bigger gestures but making them more marked and distinct.

As you become more confident with your gestures, use them to give weight to the key messages in your presentation. The more your gestures accentuate your message the more confident and charismatic you will appear. Of course you aren't miming every word but using your gestures to highlight the most important points.

CONNECT WITH SUPPORTIVE AUDIENCE MEMBERS

One of the most common questions I get from those speaking to larger audiences is how do you connect with a big group? The answer is that you don't; at least not all at once.

As you are speaking connect first with those who are willing to be connected with. Find the smiling faces or those nodding encouragingly. Keep eye contact with them for slightly longer than the others — around three to five seconds will be enough. Then sweep your gaze across the rest of the audience to the next person to connect with. As you continue, the other people in the audience will be drawn into the energy exchange between you and the initial connectors.

It is a simple and powerful technique that you will have experienced many times. If you have ever noticed two people connecting with each other across a crowded bar then you have been drawn into the energy connection between two people. Don't wait until you are presenting to a large group to practise this for the first time. When in meetings try to subtly connect with those who you think are open to it. Soften your focus as you do so and just hold the connection for a moment or two then move your eye contact around the room again for a while before returning. The aim is to become comfortable with the process. When that happens you are certain to draw an audience of any size in to your presentation.

ANSWER THE FOUR QUESTIONS ANY AUDIENCE HAS

In the 1970s Dr Bernice McCarthy developed 4MAT®, a new method for helping learners learn in their preferred style. It has been used in thousands of teaching settings for over 25 years and the four core questions provide a fantastic template upon which to develop a presentation, talk or speech.

When preparing your presentation, work on the basis that your audience has one of the following four questions and set out to answer them in this suggested order:

Why?

Why should they listen? Why are they here? Why is this important and why now? This engages these audience members emotionally. If you miss this question, as many people do in formal presentations, those for whom 'why' is the most important question will tune out.

What?

What is the concept, idea or information? This may also be the detail or structure. The more academic or theoretic members of your audience will need this information.

How?

This covers the practicalities. How will this work? What is the plan? The doers in the audience need this information to be covered. They will be patient enough to wait until you have answered the 'why' and 'what' questions but they will be vociferous if you don't give them enough of the 'how'. If you have ever had a question following a presentation that started with, 'That's all very well in theory but …', you probably haven't given a strong enough 'how'.

What if?

What are the risks and possibilities of this idea, concept or proposal? Some of your audience will be naturally risk averse and want to know that you have thought about the risks and done something to negate them. Others will be possibility-focused and will have immediate thoughts about how this can be developed, expanded or moved on. Show your audience that you have considered these but try not to be derailed by giving huge amounts of detail to the 'what ifs'.

Highly confident presenters and speakers tend to have a basic structure that they develop their content around. I highly recommend this as yours. You can use it just in the introduction, in the main body or in both. Take time to notice the positive impact of using the structure to anchor your confidence further.

Putting it all together

The biggest barrier standing in the way of most people becoming confident speakers and presenters is the thoughts they have about speaking and presenting. Many people see it as one of the biggest challenges they will face. Seeing the absurdity of these thoughts will create the biggest shift in your confidence in these situations. Enhancing your vocal and physiological skills becomes easy when seeing presenting as easy or even enjoyable.

In other chapters of this book I have shared strategies about the value of simple breathing techniques and using the whole of your vocal power. I would highly recommend marrying these with the strategies in this chapter. Together they will provide the foundation for you to become a highly proficient and confident presenter and speaker.

As you develop your skill and certainty, I would recommend that you take opportunities to speak to as wide a variety of audiences as possible. This will prevent you from falling into the trap of thinking you're confident presenting to some groups and not others. As you already know, confidence is transferable and so are speaking skills. The only thing that impacts your ability to speak to one audience over another is your thinking about the audience.

42 The confident sportsman

> ❝ There may be people that have more talent than you, but there's no excuse for anyone to work harder than you do. Derek Jeter

> ❝ Champions keep playing until they get it right. Billie Jean King

> ❝ If you fail to prepare, you're prepared to fail. Mark Spitz

> ❝ You've got to take the initiative and play your game. In a decisive set, confidence is the difference. Chris Evert

> ❝ What to do with a mistake: recognize it, admit it, learn from it, forget it. Dean Smith

While this chapter is primarily aimed at those who play competitive sport, the lessons from it are relevant to anyone who has to deliver moments of peak performance in any area of life. By peak performance I mean specific times when you need to be at your best and draw on some specific skills to deliver a result. This could be in a high-challenge meeting or interview, or in a dramatic performance, or any situation that requires you to draw on previous training.

Sport is one of the most obvious environments that confidence and the lack of it is seen and felt. When athletes lose form, quite often it is confidence that isn't present. This prevents the athlete from tapping into their training and allowing their body to do what it has been prepared for. Take professional football as an example. Most players will have been passing the ball since they were five or six years old. Professional players train for three to four hours most days of the week and play at least once a week. Despite this, most players will go through a spell where they misplace passes and struggle to do the basics of the game to the standard they should. It looks like their ability and sometimes even their energy has been sucked from their body. Clearly this isn't the case but we probably all have that sensation that we just aren't able to do things that we know we have the capability to. It is a huge confidence drain.

This chapter will help you to take back control of the mental processes that can lead to these dips in performance. My work in sport has given me access to some talented athletes but also some of the most mentally strong people I have met in any walk of life. The application of their strategies will help anyone who wants to make the most of their potential.

TRUST YOURSELF

Graeme Carrick has a unique view on football. He was a highly rated midfielder and a graduate of West Ham United's acclaimed youth academy. In his early 20s his playing career was ended by injuries. He has continued to work in the game he loves and is currently a highly rated national Grassroots Coach. As well as being a respected coach he has the unique perspective of watching older brother Michael's career blossom with Manchester United and England. Graeme is a student of the game and has just completed a Masters in Sports Coaching.

Carrick is clear that trusting yourself is a crucial part of maintaining your confidence. 'As a player you know what your best routine is. It is important to stick with this even when performances aren't at the level you would want. Everyone is different, everyone knows what their best approach is. Even on match days you will have developed a pattern that is right for you. Minimize the impact that external factors have on this routine. Towards the end of my playing career my confidence was at its lowest when I couldn't trust my body to do what it needed to. That's when I knew I had to retire. As a coach I see it as part of my job to pick up on players' routines and allow them to maintain them as the foundations of their performance.'

I share Graeme's belief that you should trust yourself and the abilities you have developed. Your job is to relax enough that your body can do what it has been trained to do. Over-thinking doesn't help. It can be much more useful to distract your mind than making extravagant changes to your approach.

During a confidential coaching session with a cricketer, he told me that when he broke into the England squad he was told he should change his whole approach to the game. He was asked to tone down the way he spoke to colleagues and even had to change how he warmed up for games. It was made clear that if he didn't he might not remain in the squad. Unfortunately as he made the changes his performance level dipped and he was left out due to a lack of runs.

Following our session he decided to be himself more. He was careful not to upset others and explained why he prepared in the way that he did, but he stuck to his routines and approaches. Naturally his form returned and he had a successful spell on the side. It is always important to trust your approach and not change it at the first downturn in performance.

KEEP THE BIG PICTURE IN MIND

James O'Connor is currently a player coach of successful US soccer team Orlando City. As of 2015 the franchise will be part of the MLS (the top tier for professional soccer in the US) and is one of the most successful teams in the history of the US Soccer League. O'Connor's playing career in the UK saw him make 554 appearances for West Bromwich Albion, Stoke City, Sheffield Wednesday and Burnley. He also holds the highest coaching qualification in Europe, the UEFA Pro Licence.

O'Connor's number one message for sporting confidence is to keep focused on the big picture.

> The goals I had for my career remained the same for ten years, yet when I went through spells when my confidence was low it would coincide with getting overly focused on smaller, less important challenges. Always keep the end goal in mind and ask yourself, "Is what I am doing helping me to

get closer to my end goal?" This approach helped me to make good choices about my health, fitness and my mental attitude. I didn't achieve everything that I wanted to in my career in England but I can be satisfied that I did everything that I could along the way. I can't imagine how much people must regret not doing everything they can to make the most of their potential.' Graeme Carrick agrees. He believes that keeping the big picture in mind will help you to manage the perceptual challenges: 'If your confidence is low your focus tends to narrow too much. You concentrate too much on the detail and don't see the big picture. Keep the big picture in mind. Focus on the overall job in hand and what you want to achieve.

FRAME MISTAKES USEFULLY

Carrick also believes that framing mistakes usefully is crucial as you build and maintain your confidence. 'One of the differentials of highly confident people I have played with and coached is that they keep mistakes in perspective. They don't dwell on errors for too long. We have to see them as opportunities to learn. No matter what level you play or perform at you will slip-up at some point. Learn what you need to and then move on to the next thing you can do to move you towards your big picture.'

James O'Connor suggests three simple questions to help you to frame mistakes usefully:

1. What do I need to do to make sure the right thing happens next time?
2. What can I learn from this?
3. Can anyone support me in avoiding this mistake in the future?

He suggests asking these simple questions, answering them, then mentally leaving the error behind.

If you watch the top players over the years they make a mistake then are willing to put themselves in the same position again. I have played against some great players and they were all willing to push themselves to be in challenging situations and take risks even if they had made an error. This feeds confidence rather than being a result of it. Dwelling on mistakes makes you fearful and seriously inhibits performance.

Putting it all together

The experiences of Carrick and O'Connor give another layer of strategies to build and maintain confidence in the sporting arena and beyond. Their experiences playing, working and, in Graeme's case, growing up with athletes at the very top of their profession makes them well qualified to give an insight into confidence in sport.

My personal experience has shown me that confidence will increase technical ability significantly. Ability without confidence will never flourish. In order to perform at your best you must also take care of the environmental factors that affect performance. On regular occasions that I am called in to work with a player who is struggling mentally I find someone who isn't sleeping or eating well. These things must be corrected alongside any interventions to increase confidence or any other mental ability.

If you are fortunate enough to have the talent to perform at a good level in any sport, take every advantage you can to make the most of that talent. Confidence is a crucial factor. Alone it will not help you to realize your potential but alongside great technical and physical development it will help you to reach your personal heights.

The confident comedian

> *The intelligent man finds almost everything ridiculous, the sensible man hardly anything.* Johann Wolfgang von Goethe

> *If life must not be taken too seriously, then so neither must death.* Samuel Butler

> *I take the work seriously, just not myself in it.* Henry Rollins

> *Don't take yourself too seriously. You have to learn not to be dismayed at making mistakes. No human being can avoid failures.* Father Lawrence G. Lovasik

> *I was irrevocably betrothed to laughter, the sound of which has always seemed to me the most civilized music in the world.* Peter Ustinov

> *One of the first muscles to contract when we laugh is the anal sphincter.* C.W. Medcalf

There are few things that require more confidence than going on stage with the job of making people laugh. Being funny to a roomful of people who are expecting to find you hilarious is daunting to say the least. One of my early teachers in the art of presence and charisma was Kevin Cherry. As well as being an esteemed business consultant, he is a lay preacher and a performer with the He-Ha's improvised comedy troupe. Having come to comedy as a profession late in life, he is well placed to guide us through comedy's lessons on confidence.

The comedian Demetri Martin points out that your true identity as far as others are concerned is the second thing people say to identify you at work or at parties. You know:

'Demitri Martin' (the first thing)

'Who?'

'The geeky one with the bowl haircut' (the second thing).

'Oh, yeah.'

Take a moment to reflect on what the second thing people say about you is.

It doesn't matter what your self-image, USP or elevator pitch is, your social or work circle will have their own 'second thing' to identify you and you have little control over that. I simply can't alter the fact I am 'the short Scottish one' in most situations in which I'm involved.

But what has this to do with confidence?

Well, we don't generally mind that period of incompetence we all experience when learning a new skill until we have to present the fruits of our labour in public (e.g. give a presentation, play a competitive game of golf, start a conversation with a stranger). We might experience frustration, even anger, but these are nothing compared to the heady cocktail of disappointment, awkwardness and downright shame we feel when failing publicly. Consciously or otherwise we are concerned about that 'second thing' we are creating. Here are my experiences and strategies for dealing with this experience in a confident way.

CHANGE YOUR 'SECOND THING'

The unconfident response we have in these situations is a learned response and can therefore be unlearned. In their book *The Improv Handbook*, Deborah Frances-White and Tom Salinsky point out that most children's goal is to have 'as many turns as possible' and often use this to measure their success rather than quality of performance. This approach is by definition childish. And yet it is such a confident approach to learning something new.

As adults, more often than not, we want to sit back and assess whether we'll be any good at something before we even give it a go (certainly in public). This process strikes me as both highly inefficient and geared to promote 'failure'.

Young children do not share our fear of appearing ridiculous or silly. This gives them a great advantage when it comes to confidently learning and practising new skills. Think about it, when in your life did you learn most and when in your life was learning effortless and even fun? Because children apply this process to life in general they are always learning rather than languishing in self-doubt or self-consciousness.

Secondly, this demonstrates it is not the *first thing* (fear, going blank, making a mistake) it's the *second thing*, how we define or name that thing, which undermines our confidence. So the classic adult pattern goes something like:

'Gone blank.'

'Who?'

'You know, the one that makes you blush uncontrollably and dig yourself into an ever deeper pit of self-loathing.'

'Oh, him.'

Sound familiar? Well it is time to change your 'second thing' descriptors because it's not what you feel that's important, it's what you feel about what you feel.

Now it would of course be mischievous of me to suggest that you can trade your terror for excitement simply by changing what you call it, so that is exactly what I'm going to do.

For example:

'Gone blank.'

'Who?'

'You know the one that makes you smile to yourself and get really creative.'

'Oh her, of course.'

Identify your 'second thing' label. Develop some alternative labels and test-run them in a number of mental rehearsals. Whatever works best, take it with you into the live environment and practise, practise, practise.

LEARN TO BE OK WITH NOT BEING OK

If you are human and you interact with other humans, then you are going to mess up. You will find yourself out of your depth. You will miss the point or get the wrong end of the wrong stick at some point. Believe it or not these moments are not your downfall. It's what you do with them that count.

Build your tolerance to these moments by having more of them. To begin with find a safe, non-judgemental environment to do so. I found this initially in Physical Theatre Training (particularly clowning) and subsequently have honed it doing improv (improvised comedy) to paying audiences. It's not that you can't fail (though some improv trainers will say you can't), it's more that your audience love it when (in the words of John Wright in *Why is that so funny*) you are in the shit. It's an expected part of the deal.

Find something you have the capacity to learn but that will stretch, challenge and make you feel awkward (that last one is important) during the learning process. This builds a tolerance and comfort with 'not being OK'.

For me this process has performed a kind of lobotomy in that it has surgically separated confidence and capability. Just because I lack capability in an area doesn't mean I have to relinquish confidence in myself. Perhaps ironically this 'isolated' confidence tends to allow me to develop capability more quickly and less painfully.

STOP TAKING YOURSELF SO DAMN SERIOUSLY

Practise seeing the funny side of every situation (even if you don't share it with your audience, the board or the judge). One way to practise this when the stakes are low is to ask the question, 'What could this mean?' rather than 'What does this mean?' This is what observational comedians do when they find new ways of framing familiar situations to find the fun in them.

Let me give you a personal example. I have recently been suffering from an on-going urological problem which has gone undiagnosed and not really treated effectively. It was really getting me down and affecting my more general health and sense of wellbeing. An Eastern European consultant proved to be my saviour, but not in the way you might think. He conducted the kind of invasive examination that is the stuff of a man's nightmares, inserting a camera where a camera really ought not to go (are your eyes watering yet?). He discovered, nothing.

However his letter to my GP proved a turning point in my attitude to the illness and my general wellbeing. The words 'Mr Cherry's external genitalia are unremarkable' made me laugh out loud for the first time in months. It had the same effect on many of my Facebook friends.

As C.W. Medcalf says 'taking your challenge seriously and yourself lightly' opens up many possibilities for ourselves and invites others unconsciously to join us. Smiling is thought to be one of the few universal languages.

Putting it all together

The word 'silly' has over many centuries taken a fascinating journey through a range of evolving meanings. 'Silly' did not originally refer to the absurd or ridiculous – in fact quite the opposite. The word derives from the old English word 'seely', meaning happy, blissful, lucky or blessed. From there it came to mean innocent, or deserving of compassion, only later mutating this sense of naive childishness into a more critical, mocking term, signifying ignorance, feeble-mindedness, and foolish behaviour – the meaning we know today.

My lessons about confidence from comedy can be summarized in three key points:

- Feel what you feel without judging yourself. It is the 'second thing' that matters.
- Build your 'in the shit' muscle and make tricky business like business as usual.
- Face it we are ridiculous. Most of our social constructs, if we had to explain them to a Martian (or even a child) are made up, arbitrary and frankly ridiculous. Accept that and those awkward moments will lose all of their sting.

Professor A Nalsphinctre (aka Kevin Cherry, Agent Improvocateur)

44 The confident teacher

> *Education breeds confidence. Confidence breeds hope. Hope breeds peace.* Confucius

> *By learning you will teach; by teaching you will understand.* Latin proverb

> *It is the supreme art of the teacher to awaken joy in creative expression and knowledge.* Albert Einstein

> *A master can tell you what he expects of you. A teacher, though, awakens your own expectations.* Patricia Neal

> *You cannot teach a man anything, you can only help him find it within himself.* Galileo Galilei

'Teaching is the worst job in the world but the greatest vocation.'

Joanne Nugent is a former head of history in a challenging area of the north-east of England. In her role as Extended Schools Consultant she has coached and enabled hundreds of teachers, parents and vulnerable teenagers to develop their confidence and self-esteem. She is also your coach for this chapter.

As a young and enthusiastic trainee teacher at one the finest educational establishments in England, I was greeted with the above statement during my induction. For me teaching was my destiny. There was nothing I wanted to do more and for someone to suggest that it was a terrible job was baffling to say the least. Yes I was young and very wet behind the ears

but I was enthusiastic and determined to be a great teacher.
Clearly I had a lot to learn. Teaching isn't all motherhood
and apple pie. It challenges you mentally, emotionally and
physically. It forces you to question your values, your belief
system and your self-worth. The expectations of you as a
teacher are high. Your headteacher, head of department,
parents, social workers, community police, your pupils and the
media all expect teachers to be more than great. Perfection
is the requirement and to be void of mistakes.

High expectations are essential to raising standards. However,
such expectations in an ever-changing profession can
demoralize and chip away at the confidence of any teacher
no matter how enthusiastic or experienced they are. The
pressure to perform and to prove that you have added value
can make you question your place in the profession.

A number of headteachers have asked me over the years
to help, support and coach teachers who they feel lack
confidence. As a teacher it is difficult to admit you need help
or that you are not this all-singing, all-dancing performer who
has every pupil eating out of the palm of your hand! The
single most important point to note is that great teachers
are not born they are made. So much emphasis is placed
upon raising the confidence and self-belief of young people.
However, unless we place the same value and importance
upon raising the confidence of our teaching staff we will lose
great talent and our children will suffer.

BE THE CONFIDENT TEACHER YOUR PUPILS NEED

I have encouraged many teachers to use this technique as the
starting point to develop their confidence. It is a great way to
hold the mirror up to your own behaviours and their impact
on your students' confidence. Write a list of all of the habits and
dispositions you want your pupils to have by the end of the
year, or whatever time span you will be working with them for.

The list often include such qualities as:

- To be enthusiastic about life.
- To have a hunger for learning.
- To be tenacious.
- To learn from mistakes.
- To learn from others.
- To ask questions about their learning.
- To be happy.
- To feel safe and confident in the classroom.
- To feel successful.
- To believe in themselves.
- To know what they are good at/where their strengths lie.

After reviewing the list, flip it to give you the behaviours you must demonstrate most. It is important to accept that unless you display those qualities your pupils won't. As hard as it may be to accept, you have to be a model for your pupils. That includes modelling enthusiasm, being tenacious and believing in yourself.

Use this as the basis of your personal development planning. If any of these aren't natural to you then what needs to happen for you to make them so?

FOCUS ON BEHAVIOUR MANAGEMENT

How often have you thought 'Year 9 are out of control,' or, 'My Year 11 class will not listen and they are so lazy'. Teachers rarely get the opportunity to just talk about their experiences or what happens in their classroom. If you are having a problem with a particular pupil or class then the chances are so will others. Try to seek out a friend or a colleague whom you trust or at least respect. A number of professions offer their staff supervision. This is not performance management but an informal opportunity to discuss your work and air your worries or concerns without the fear that you are failing or are incapable. I have worked with a number of schools that operate under challenging circumstances and they have implemented such an approach. They have noted several positive outcomes, such as a reduction in staff sickness, higher retention of staff, more purposeful and enthusiastic staff meetings and a happier staffroom.

If your environment doesn't provide this support, I would highly recommend being brave and videoing yourself teaching. Many people fear this, but it is hugely beneficial. Video your favourite class or your favourite subject and watch it through twice. The first time watch and enjoy the lesson. The second time make a note of the atmosphere in the classroom, the relationship between you and the pupils, and how disruptions in the classroom are dealt with. Focus on positives not negatives. Having done this, video yourself with your worst class. Again watch it through twice then compare and contrast their performance in both videos. The results are often very enlightening.

Be ready to notice yourself mirroring the behaviour of the children. For example, I have often coached teachers who noticed that they were primed for bad behaviour so they could pounce on it immediately and as a result they made the situation worse. Focus on rebuilding the rapport between you and the more challenging class. Remember just as 'great' teachers are not born neither are 'great classes'.

PREPARE

Confident teachers plan and prepare their lessons. No matter how qualified you are or how many years you have been teaching, planning and preparation are essential to the success of you and your pupils. If you are teaching a subject that you don't fully understand or enjoy, you have to work harder to make sure that you are comfortable with the subject matter and that your delivery is enthusiastic and effortless. Odd as it seems these are often your most memorable lessons.

If you are given a lesson plan, be sure to make it your own. You will get greater results if you take ownership of it. What would bring the subject to life for you? What would make it easy for you to understand?

Beyond that, be sure to remain consistently prepared for the role. Always keep up with current educational research and theories about learning. Research the internet and be keen to attend training courses. There are many key strategies that thousands of teachers believe have transformed their teaching and the learning of their pupils. Don't ignore or dismiss what others say is working for them. Their strategies could work for you too and you could enjoy yourself in the process. Just because we are teachers does not mean that we are not learners.

This may seem very obvious but over the years some of my most unwilling learners have been teachers. Be a magpie and take from others what you need or want and it will make you feel confident. Surround yourself with successful members of staff, those who enjoy and achieve. Don't be dragged down by negativity or sourness.

Putting it all together

To become a confident teacher you need to consistently keep focused on why you became a teacher in the first place. Headteachers or heads of departments will come and go as quickly as education secretaries, but you must know what your core beliefs and values are. This clarity will impact upon the effectiveness of your teaching and the learning of your pupils more than anything else. You expect high standards from your pupils. Demand the same high standards of yourself. Be the best teacher you can be. Know where your strengths lie. Understand what works for you and what works for your pupils. Do what needs to be done. If something isn't working do something about it, change it. Do something you are proud of. There will be bumps in the road. There will be obstacles that you struggle to climb over. Don't get stuck. Find a new route and get round it.

45 The confident learner

> *If we learned how to walk and talk the way we are taught how to read and write – everybody would limp and stutter.* Mark Twain

> *Don't let the fear of striking out hold you back.* Babe Ruth

> *There are two mistakes one can make along the road to truth – not going all the way, and not starting.* Buddha

> *Strength does not come from physical capacity. It comes from an indomitable will.* Mahatma Gandhi

> *Nothing builds self-esteem and self-confidence like accomplishment.* Thomas Carlyle

When you think about learning what image do you conjure up? Is it a classroom with a teacher hosing you with information while you struggle to keep up? Perhaps it is a training course with the trainer practising death by PowerPoint as you strive to stay focused and awake? Or do you think of a joyful and energetic experience where you interact with others and explore information that is relevant and easy to apply?

For all too many people the former examples are true. Education can be an unpleasant requirement of life and because much of our formal education takes place during our most formative years this struggle leads to a long-term impact on our confidence. My younger brother was neither academic in the traditional way nor enjoyed sports or the arts. School was extremely tough for him and building relationships was difficult because he wasn't naturally included in the pursuits of others. He left school having been bullied throughout and with very little in the way of qualifications and even less confidence. Yet now he holds a steady job in financial services involved in rock bands. How can this happen? My experience suggests it is because most approaches to learning and education are hugely out-dated. Our education system is founded on principles that are over a century old and the targets that many teachers and trainers are set lead to an approach that isolates many modern-day learners.

I am incredibly fortunate to have worked with a visionary in the field of learning who changed my view on learning and life forever. Kimberley Hare is the Managing Director of Kaizen Training and has been voted one of the world's most influential people in the field of Accelerated Learning. It is with huge thanks to her that I share three strategies to help build confidence through learning more quickly and elegantly. If you are a teacher, trainer or consultant I would highly recommend her book *The Trainer's Toolkit: Bringing Brain-friendly Learning to Life*. If you are in business, are a parent or just want to keep learning then use these to make your learning journey easier and more enjoyable.

DISCOVER YOUR SMARTS

One of the most profound discoveries that I have made in my years as a trainer was the work of Dr Howard Gardner and his coding of multiple intelligences. Dr Gardner and his colleagues found that the notion of IQ was both limited and out-dated. IQ really focuses only on mathematical and verbal linguistic ability and this is only a fraction of the picture.

After many years of research Dr Gardner asserted that there are eight ways in which we are all intelligent. These are:

- Visual Spatial
- Interpersonal
- Intrapersonal
- Musical Rhythmic
- Verbal Linguistic
- Mathematical Logical
- Bodily Kinaesthetic
- Naturalist

For more of a description of each of these read Dr Gardner's paper 'In a nutshell' (listed in Further reading).

Perhaps even more important than understanding the intelligences in-depth is the appreciation that:

1. We are all intelligent in different ways. The question is not, 'How smart are you?' but instead, 'How are you smart?'
2. Potential is not fixed. All intelligence is developable.
3. You can develop any intelligence through any of the others.

Armed with this knowledge you can naturally and easily become a more confident learner. If I apply this knowledge to my younger brother's experience again, we now know he could use his musical rhythmic intelligence to develop the more traditionally academic verbal linguistic and visual spatial. Which intelligence that you are naturally high in could you use to develop the others?

It is almost impossible to only develop one intelligence at a time. When James joined his first band then the academic intelligences increased as expected but his interpersonal intelligence naturally developed because he was spending more time with more people. As he practised his music more, his musical intelligence grew yet stronger.

Knowing and understanding that you are smart in various ways and that your intelligence can be continually developed is a great first step to becoming a confident learner.

START WITH THE END IN MIND

A major flaw in the traditional approach to education is that much of it seems to be a means to an end. The brilliant Sir Ken Robinson captures this brilliantly in his 2006 TED Talk on how schools kill creativity (see Further reading for details of this).

If you were to visit education as an alien and say, 'What's it for, public education?', I think you'd have to conclude, if you look at the output, who really succeeds by this, who does everything they should, who gets all the brownie points, who are the winners, I think you'd have to conclude the whole purpose of public education throughout the world is to produce university professors.

The challenge reaches beyond education into corporate training. Most people get their list of training courses that they can attend and choose some because we are told that we should want to develop.

Stepping into becoming a confident learner is to become brilliant at defining your learning outcomes. Specifically this means being able to get absolutely clear on what you want to be able to do differently as a result of the learning you are going to do. How will you know it has been a success? How will the relevant people around you know?

This additional clarity will help you to become much more discerning in the learning that you do but also to help you recognize your progress much more easily. All training courses should be designed with outcomes (not just training objectives) at their heart. If you are able to, challenge any that aren't.

REFLECT ON YOUR LEARNING

In a world where most learning is a means to an end it is completely understandable that we finish a course, pick up a certificate and never think about it again. However the highly confident learner will reflect on learning experiences from the most powerful to the most disappointing. They will do it whether that learning was in a formal setting like a training course, or self-managed learning online or from a book.

Great reflective questions to ask include:

- What worked? Why?
- What didn't work? Why?
- What will this help me to do differently?
- How can I share this experience with others?
- What else do I need to do differently as a result of this experience?

The habit of **reflections** helps to anchor the learning and reinforces a self-perception that you are **learning** and a good one at that? To build this habit will also wire your brain to recognize that you are important because you and others have invested in your learning.

One final recommendation would be to have a specific book for your reflections. This provides a brilliant resource for review in the future and becomes a superb reminder that you are a font of knowledge.

Putting it all together

It is hard to separate learning in its broader sense from confidence, as we understand it. The challenge for many of us is that we have been conditioned into thinking we aren't good at learning. As human beings we are naturally predisposed to learning. Perhaps the two most difficult things that we ever learn to do – walking and talking – happen in the most instinctive way. Sadly the learning systems that have been in place throughout recent history and beyond get in the way of our natural approach.

By applying the three strategies in this chapter you undoubtedly take a more natural approach to learning which in turn will help you to access your confidence more easily. In turn feeling more genuinely confident more of the time will help you to learn more naturally and stay away from experiences that will hold less value.

Learning, when done well, should be stretching and challenging and ultimately rewarding. At times it will also be fun. While enjoyment must be part of the journey it is important to remember that highly confident people will often embark on learning experiences that aren't necessarily fun at the time because these can be the most rewarding. As your confidence grows, be sure to embrace learning that both builds on your strengths and grows the areas you need to develop most.

46 The confident body

I share the same advice that my mom gave me – stay hydrated and sleep well. And that being a beautiful person on the inside is what really matters. Jessica Alba

I've never felt a push to be stick thin. I work out and eat healthy, so mostly it's about being in shape and having energy. Lauren Conrad

To lose confidence in one's body is to lose confidence in oneself. Simone de Beauvoir

Take care of your body. It's the only place you have to live. Jim Rohn

By choosing healthy over skinny you are choosing self-love over self-judgment. You are beautiful! Steve Maraboli

No matter how practised we become at triggering confidence from the inside out it is difficult to ignore the impact of feeling good about your body. I am not talking about the need for defined abs or toned butts but the benefits of genuine confidence in being in our own skin. For the past couple of years I have worked closely with Performance Enhancement Specialist Nick Grantham. Nick's clients include Premiership Football Clubs, international athletes and even Royal Ballet companies. He is one of the UK's top experts on athletic preparation and is your coach for this chapter.

How can you develop body confidence? Confidence is a feeling that we get as a result of what we think, what we do with our body and how we perceive the world around us.

Type 'A Confident Body' into a search engine and you'll be amazed by the number of results you get (within 0.24 seconds I discovered 122,000,000 links). Rather predictably, if the information at the end of a mouse click is to be believed, having a confident body is simply a matter of developing a 'bikini body' and is predominantly a problem faced by women.

First you need to forget what the internet and popular media would have you believe. Throughout my career as a performance enhancement specialist I've helped shape thousands of 'confident bodies' and I've come to realize 'a confident body' means different things to different people.

- The world champion judo player with an injured shoulder who can no longer perform his 'signature move' on opponents.
- The working mum who constantly feels exhausted at the end of the day and is longing to keep her eyes open past nine o'clock in the evening!
- The 65-year-old recreational triathlete returning to fitness following a brain tumour that left him with balance and coordination problems.
- The successful executive living through an endless cycle of corporate hospitality, who is so out of shape that he can't have a game of football with his kids in the park at the weekend.

All real-life clients that I've worked with, all looking to develop 'a confident body', and none of them wanting to walk down the beach in a bikini or pair of speedos! In each case they created structures and habits around the following three key strategies.

KEEP IT CONSISTENT

'Are you 'fit for *purpose*'? The first thing that needs to be established is what you want your body to be capable of doing, physically.

Can you run for the bus without straining a muscle? Can you play with your children in the park without having to sit on the park bench for five minutes while you catch your breath? Can you play five-a-side with the 'Class of 72' every Sunday night without aching for the next five days?

Once you've figured out what you want to be able to do, you can plan how you are going to do it. It may mean a trip to the gym a couple of times a week but it could simply be dusting off the bike in the garage and getting out for some fresh air on a regular basis. Regardless of how you go about becoming 'fit for purpose', continuity is the key to success and will help you to establish a training habit. Habits build confidence. Time-efficient programmes will help you to get the most out of everything you do. Find out what the minimum 'dose' is that delivers the maximum 'effect'.

We all lead busy lives and a 'results by volume' approach to fitness training is inefficient and a bit dull. A 15-minute training session completed four times a week will form a stronger habit than a 60-minute session completed once a week. Continuity and efficiency are fundamental aspects of developing a successful physical preparation programme to enable you to develop a confident body.

EAT WELL AND HYDRATE

What would happen if Lewis Hamilton's pit crew decided to fill up with a few gallons of diesel instead of the sophisticated fuel blend they usually use? He wouldn't get out of the pit lane. Yet this is precisely what we do on a daily basis.

The body is a pretty sophisticated piece of kit that needs the right balance of nutrients to perform optimally. The adaptations that will allow you to develop a confident body can only occur when the body is fuelled appropriately.

Let's take a quick quiz to gauge your nutritional knowledge.

1. What is better for you, a chocolate muffin or an apple?
2. What is better for you, a can of fizzy drink or a glass of water?
3. What is better for you, a side portion of chips or a side portion of seasonal vegetables?
4. What is better for you, a takeaway pizza or a home-cooked meal using fresh ingredients?

You already have all the nutritional knowledge that you need. I'm not about to suggest you go on a 'mung bean superfood milkshake diet'. Establishing nutritional habits to help develop a confident body requires structure. Make appropriate food choices and stick to a plan. Concentrate on getting the basics right:

- Eat regularly.
- Limit sugars, and refined and highly processed food.
- Eat fruits and vegetables.
- Drink more water (2.5 litres a day).
- Consume lean proteins.

MAKE RECOVERY IMPORTANT

Many of the issues related to poor body confidence are linked to chronic fatigue. I wouldn't expect my athletes to train 60–80 hours a week, 50 weeks of the year without a rest, so why are you any different? I've worked with successful executives and stay-at-home mums who have shown all the signs of 'overtraining' yet they've not worked out in years! If the body cannot cope with the physical and mental demands of what life has to throw at it, it will quickly become exhausted.

Sleep is one of the most important forms of recovery and provides time for adaptation and recovery.

Try to establish a regular sleep pattern and aim for eight to ten hours of good-quality sleep each night. If you like to burn the midnight oil, remember that the hours before midnight are far more valuable for recovery and regeneration (every hour of sleep before midnight is equal to two hours of sleep after midnight).

Create an effective sleep environment:

Relax. Use relaxation skills to switch off; turn the TV and electronic devices off.

Quiet. Use ear plugs, place 'do not disturb' signs on doors, switch phones to silent.

Dark. Reduce light in the room 30 minutes before going to sleep, wear an eye mask. Keep the room cool – 18°C/65°F is the optimal temperature.

Comfort. Make sure you've got room to manoeuvre!'

Putting it all together

The basis of Nick's advice may be common sense to some, but is it your common practice? As he is at pains to point out, 'A confident body is being secure in the knowledge that whatever it is you want your body to do (run for the bus, play with the grandchildren, complete a charity 5km run or simply make it to 8pm without falling asleep) you can achieve it by sticking to the basics and developing habits around a comprehensive physical preparation programme and sound nutrition strategy, while remembering to take some time out to relax and unwind'.

We have been mutual clients over the years, with him getting me in better physical shape and me working with him to develop his business strategy. In one of our first meetings I asked him the best way to lose weight and his response was to 'burn more energy than you consume'. No shocks there, other than the realization that I had to change my eating and/or exercise habits.

Similarly most of us know that we should drink the 2.5 litres of water a day that Nick recommends, but how many of us actually do it? I have worked with clients whose confidence levels have increased just by getting their water intake to a healthy level. They reported feeling more lucid and having more energy.

Until recently Nick's website (www.nickgrantham.com) displayed the Miles Kington quote: 'Knowledge is knowing that a tomato is a fruit. Wisdom is knowing that a tomato doesn't belong in a fruit salad.' Use the core information in this chapter as part of your confidence platform. Your goal may be to recreate *Baywatch*, but once your are clear on what it is then take simple and consistent steps to achieve it.

47 The confident courter

❝ *Courting is a much sweeter term than 'dating'. It sounds like it has more intent, more like an agreement that two people enter into with a future in mind.* Kim Cattrall

❝ *Keep love in your heart. A life without it is like a sunless garden when the flowers are dead.* Oscar Wilde

❝ *It's fun to have a partner who understands your life and lets you be you.* Kim Kardashian

❝ *When you stop trying to find the right man and start becoming the right woman, the right man will find his way to you.* Cher

❝ *It sounds like a cliché but I also learnt that you're not going to fall for the right person until you really love yourself and feel good about who you are.* Emma Watson

This chapter is for everyone, not just those who haven't found Mr or Miss Right yet. Imagine how many failing relationships could have been salvaged over the years if those in them were willing to go back and revisit some basic dating principles. Unless you are 100 per cent happy with your relationship, then I would encourage you to read on.

For those of you who are still looking for a great relationship, there should be no surprise in learning that confidence plays a key role. I am sure that you have had the 'how have they ended up with them' conversation in your head many times as someone you watch, someone who is highly attractive, leaves a club or party with someone much less attractive. It is especially infuriating if their date appears to have confidence that outstrips their physical attributes and even their personality. I am not saying confidence is everything, but genuine confidence is unquestionably attractive.

It is also worth deciding before you read further what kind of date you are looking for. If you are younger you might want to read this chapter to help you get the most attractive or cool date that you can. As long as you stay safe that is all good with me! If you are slightly older you might be looking for a life partner. While physical attraction is crucial in any relationship your awareness that beauty is wasted on the young comes to the fore. You want more than the prettiest, best dressed or fittest. You will identify more with the quote: 'More girls need to be infatuated by a man with an education, ambition, faith and goals rather than a dude with 'swag'. In ten years swag won't pay your bills.' While the incredibly hot high school date or holiday romance could turn into the partner you spend your life with, it is quite rare. If you're looking for a good time don't rule out everyone who isn't an intellectual genius and if you are looking for a father for your children don't date gorgeous slobs. Whatever relationship you are looking for here are three strategies that I have observed in the most confident daters I have studied.

PAY FULL ATTENTION

Think about the last date you went on. Think of the person you were with. What were they wearing when you met? What was the most personal thing they told you about themselves? If you were going to date them again what information from your previous time together could you use to start conversations and show that you are interested?

The most significant difference between highly confident daters and the rest is that they pay full attention. Strategies for connecting and really listening are already covered in other areas of the book but when dating there is something extra at play. You are paying attention for what really seems to matter most to the person you are wooing.

238

This information doesn't come from a single obvious source. It comes from small subtle sources and quiet messages. If you are focused on the self-talk that is chatting inside you or on working out what you are going to say next then you will miss them. Depending where your date is taking place, the environment or your date's friends can be an incredibly useful source of information. Being able to ask a question about something you have noticed and prompting your date to talk about it is the number one way to be seen as interesting. It is a myth that you have to have interesting stories to tell. The secret is to create the opportunity for them to tell interesting stories and then to really pay attention to everything they are saying.

BE YOU ... AT YOUR BEST

Having read this book and applied the techniques this should be both easier and more obvious. Let us just assume for a moment that your dating approach and date selection is so successful that you find someone who you want to be with long term. This is doomed to failure if you try to be someone you aren't in the honeymoon stages of the relationship. I have friends who would invent hobbies and interests to impress the opposite sex. I have even more who have deleted hobbies and interests so as not to scare off a potential partner. Many of the friends that I have I have met through playing football. In our younger days so many teammates would complain that their now serious girlfriend was trying to stop them from playing. This was rarely down to an over-controlling girlfriend but much more often down to a lack of honesty by the guy involved in the early part of the relationship.

Being you at your best stretches much further and deeper than being honest about how you spend your time. It includes but isn't limited to:

- Being well dressed and well turned out but in the style you are comfortable in.
- Taking your dates to the best of the places you know. Don't go to wildly extravagant places if you aren't comfortable or try to be a cultural expert if you aren't.

- Talk about things you are really interested in, in moderation (unless you know for sure that they are interested in them too.) Passion about any topic is attractive. Having a date go on endlessly about something you find dull isn't. There is no point trying to hide the things you're interested in altogether though. Unless of course you are prepared to do so forever.

THE BALANCE BETWEEN INTERESTED AND DESPERATE

I am sure at some point in your life you will have had the experience of being pursued by someone you really were not interested in. It can be cute and flattering, unless they seem desperate. In which case it is incredibly unattractive and uncomfortable. If at any point in your dating journey you feel desperate to be with someone you should stop dating and start working on your confidence in other areas of your life. Desperation is repellent to all but to all but the worst potential suitors.

The flipside of that is that most people you date want you to show that you are interested in them. I recall fondly the first time that I met my wife. Her friends were getting ready to move on to the next party and, having been engrossed in conversation for about an hour, it was clear that one of us had to make the big move of asking for the other's number. I took the plunge first. Looking back on that first meeting, I once asked her what she would have done if I hadn't asked. She replied that she would have left it until she was about to walk out the door to ask, 'Don't you want my number?' This is a classic 'check-out' of interest.

One of my best friend's mantras when he was dating was 'play it cool Trigger', a reference to a famous scene from UK sitcom *Only Fools and Horses*. At the moment the lead character is trying to play it cool he loses the chance to impress his potential date. It is a great metaphor and leads to a great question to ask yourself when dating. How would you want to them to show they were keen but not desperately so? What does the right balance look like for you?

Putting it all together

Beginning a new relationship is a challenging and exciting time. Even if your aim is to find Mr or Miss Right Now, rather than the person you will spend the rest of your life with, the road is a bumpy one. That road can be smoothed by applying the foundations of confidence overlaid with some specific strategies that will keep you connected with your potential suitor.

The core principle of being seen as interesting by being interested is crucial in the early stages of dating. 'Watch, listen and remember' should be the mantra. Put your full attention on them and their environment. Find out what interests them, what is important to them and what you have in common. Make this the foundation of any future relationship.

Show up to the early dates – and beyond – as the best, most confident version of you. A date hungover from the night before is unlikely to be attractive unless you are looking for a party animal for a partner. I was once given the fantastic advice: 'Wear yourself well, but wear yourself'. Trying to be someone or something you aren't is tiring and will cause relationships to stutter in the long run.

Don't be the desperate one at 3:30am trying to hook up with anyone who is left in the nightclub. Desperation is one of the most unattractive traits and the only people you are likely to attract are those so insecure in themselves that they want to be with someone else less confident than them. Balance this with the confidence to say, 'Yes, I would like to see you again'. Playing hard to get will drive more good dates away than it attracts.

The final point of this chapter is slightly clichéd but also completely true. You will only find love when you are at peace with yourself. Don't wait for a relationship to validate you and give you confidence. Trigger your confidence and make it the state you hang out in most and the rest will take care of itself.

48 The confident relationship

> **❝** The meeting of two personalities is like the contact of two chemical substances: if there is any reaction, both are transformed. C. G. Jung

> **❝** Being deeply loved gives you strength; loving deeply gives you courage. Lao Tzu

> **❝** A dame that knows the ropes isn't likely to get tied up. Mae West

> **❝** Assumptions are the termites of relationships. Henry Winkler

> **❝** When dealing with people, remember you are not dealing with creatures of logic, but with creatures bristling with prejudice and motivated by pride and vanity. Dale Carnegie

If you skipped the previous chapter on confident dating, then congratulations on being in a strong and steady relationship. If it is a fulfilling one for you, or you want it to be, my wish is that this chapter helps you to nurture and maintain it. While not every one of the highly confident people who I have worked with or studied were in a great relationship, I do see a strong relationship as a great foundation upon which to build personal success and confidence.

A loving and intimate relationship should not be a prerequisite of confidence. In fact, that ability to access and live in your confidence before and during your relationship is much more likely to lead to that relationship being successful. However, as a species wired for contact and connection, being in a great relationship can easily be the most satisfying and fulfilling part of our lives.

Modern-day life can place obstacles in the way of these relationships being successful in the long term. Longer and less consistent working hours, the globalization of careers, a media that sets unreasonably high expectations for the physical aspects of relationships are just a few examples of the challenges we all face.

With these challenges in mind we must nurture our relationships to keep them strong. Even at those times when we doubt our relationships or partners, fostering the relationship will give us a sense of confidence. This comes either from the knowledge that we have done what we can to make it a success or from affirming love and affection from a happy and fulfilled partner.

This also seems like the perfect time to remind you that everything else in this book remains valid. Your confidence is an emotional state that you can trigger at any moment. It can be built and anchored through a whole plethora of strategies. Your confidence does not hang on the love of someone else. If you have done what you can in a relationship and your affection or commitment has not been reciprocated this does not need to affect your confidence. If it does it is because of what you are thinking about the end of that relationship.

If you are in a great relationship, here are a few strategies to maintain it.

BE PRESENT

You may be surprised to know that I don't specifically mean that you need to spend the right amount of time with your partner. I am talking quality, not just quantity. One of the attributes that I notice consistently in those people who are really confident in their relationships is that when they are spending time with their partner they are fantastic at being really present.

When spending time with your loved one, avoid distractions and clear your mind of nagging worries. Listen to and focus on what your partner is saying and doing. You will notice things that others don't.

Here are a few things to avoid in order to be present with your partner:

- **Avoid social media.** The likes of Facebook and Twitter are addictive and time consuming. A quick look can lead to a chunk of time disappearing. If you are interested in a conversation that is taking place online your focus will be drawn there even when you aren't on reading your updates
- **Use the record button.** For many people the routine at the end of the workday culminates in settling on the sofa with your partner and the TV. Unless you are watching programmes that you both enjoy and that promote conversation between you, be very careful about becoming lost in a programme and losing the opportunity to connect with your loved one.
- **Stay out of your head.** We all get lost in our thoughts at times. We have concerns that need mental attention. We have hobbies or interests that provide a mental release from day-to-day life. Date night is not the time to get lost in your thoughts. If you have something on your mind during the quality time you have with your loved one then let them know that is the case. You don't have to talk about it in-depth. Just let them know and give them permission to help you snap out of your thoughts if necessary.
- **Switch off your telephone.** Many people seem to have forgotten that if they switch their phone off they will still receive their messages when they switch it back on. If you are spending time with your partner, don't take calls unless they are genuinely urgent and ignore your messages until a more appropriate moment.

ASK FOR WHAT YOU WANT AND EXPRESS GRATITUDE

If you ever have a conversation with your partner that includes, 'You should have asked', 'Well you should have just known' then this strategy should act as a reminder that confident relationships require each partner to ask for what they want. Ask your partner to go places with you, ask them to help you make decisions, ask your partner to say or do things that fulfil you. Ask for what you want physically, mentally and emotionally.

This of course doesn't guarantee that you will but those who are confident in themselves and their relationships are completely comfortable with asking and comfortable with not getting everything they want. Relationships are much more likely to be damaged by a partner avoiding making requests and hoping that their companion guesses what they want. Great relationships are built on love and trust not mind-reading.

Showing gratitude is at least as powerful and important. In research supported by the American National Institute of Mental Health grateful couples were found to be more satisfied in their relationships and felt closer to each other. Go beyond showing gratitude for what your partner does. Be grateful for who your partner is. Show appreciation for the attributes that make them unique and especially for those that attracted you in the first place.

Be thankful for them and be overt in the ways you say and show this. Even if this isn't natural to you, create a system to remind you to show your gratitude for them.

FORGIVE FREELY

If you are in a relationship you will screw up and so will your partner. Human nature is to err. How you react to your partner's mistakes will define the relationship and your confidence in it. Highly confident people do not forgive everything but when they do forgive they do so fully and do everything that they can to leave the incident behind.

When I coach clients on challenges in their relationship there is often residue from a partner's past misdemeanour that is becoming a barrier to intimacy or communication. No matter how big or small the fault is, if you decide to move on then you must do so completely.

Bringing up past arguments and errors when your companion makes another mistake is of course damaging for the relationship. It can also have a negative impact on your confidence. By packing together all of the errors your loved one has made you will begin to question your judgement in forgiving the previous misdemeanours or being with them in the first place.

Of course there is a time to see a pattern in behaviour and end a relationship. For example if your partner has an affair then you must choose whether to forgive them. If you do you must work together to move on completely. If your partner has another affair in close succession, despite promises to change, then it is completely within reason to see this as a pattern of behaviour. Whether you forgive again is a choice you have to make, but do so with confidence in the knowledge that your relationship doesn't define you and that you have done everything you can to make it a success.

Putting it all together

Great relationships don't just happen. Even relationships that start great must be cultivated to stand the test of time. We live in times where gender roles are becoming more blurred and even the nature of same-sex relationships is changing. It is becoming easier culturally for relationships to fall apart than to be maintained.

If you want a great relationship that feels like a confident entity in itself as well as helping to foster the confidence of those in it, then you must nurture it. Confident relationships aren't hard work; at least not all the time. They do require attention especially in the midst of demands from children and careers.

If you make time to be present with your partner then you will notice all of the things they need to be emotionally satisfied and you will reap the benefits in return. Asking for what you want shows an attractive self-confidence, and regularly demonstrating gratitude shows a love and humility that will prove irresistible for the right partner. Finally, the ability to genuinely forgive your loved one for their inevitable faults and mistakes strengthens the foundations of love and trust that any long-term relationship must have.

There is no blueprint for a great relationship but a relationship fuelled by genuine confidence has the best chance to flourish and be fulfilling for everyone involved.

49) The confident parent

❝ *The more people have studied different methods of bringing up children, the more they have come to the conclusion that what good mothers and fathers instinctively feel like doing for their babies is the best after all.* Dr Benjamin Spock

❝ *Your children need your presence more than your presents.* Jesse Jackson

❝ *Your children will become what you are; so be what you want them to be.* David Bly

❝ *You don't always know what your kids will do, but your kids should always know what you will do.* Joyce Sanders

❝ *Children have more need of models than of critics.* Carolyn Coats

Becoming a parent changes your life. Being a parent becomes your life. It is a job that you do not get paid for, the hours are endless, the conditions smelly, there is no annual leave, and no professional development. Being a parent is the toughest thing you will ever do and the most important job you will ever do.

It is also the most rewarding and joyous experience of your life. It is a gift and so many people don't receive that gift but long for it every day. You want to get it right. You want to be a good parent. The pressure to be a good parent is greater now than it has ever been. Parents are told that they are their child's first and greatest teacher. Scientists and educationalists insist that the first five years of a child's life are the most important in terms of the development. They provide the foundations for a child to achieve their key developmental milestones. The brain develops more rapidly in the first three years of life than at any other stage in their life. Ninety per cent of a child's brain develops by the age of five. Does that mean if you don't get it right in the first five years all is lost? No, but it is an example of one of the pressures parents are placed under.

Not only are you raising a happy and healthy child but you have to make sure that you raise a child who has manners, morals and good hygiene. Your child must be independent, literate and an excellent communicator. We are bombarded with stories of child geniuses and world changers yet most of the pressure we feel comes from within. While confidence in our parenting skills may be difficult to maintain we now have a greater understanding of what helps children flourish and what stunts their development. We know what children respond to and how the brain in children and in teenagers develops.

WHEN YOU SAY 'NO', MEAN 'NO'

Being a parent you want to give your child the world. You want them to have anything and everything if it makes them happy. The problem arises when we give our children things to keep them quiet. It is easier to say 'yes' than to say 'no'. Parents often tell their children 'no', but how often do they mean it? The ramifications of not meaning no are huge. In the short term you may feel the consequences but the long-term consequences are on the child.

Children and teenagers know how to get you to change your mind. No matter whether it is a bar of chocolate, to use your iPhone or to be allowed to stay out late, no must mean no. This doesn't mean no until they create such a scene, cry their eyes out or be sufficiently mean to you that you feel guilty and give in. This creates an unhealthy pattern for you and them.

Firstly they will know that your word is not to be trusted. When you want them to do as they are told, such as when you are out and about, they will take no notice of you as they know they can get round you. The child will appear spoilt and you will be embarrassed.

Secondly it is very important that the child or teenager accepts 'no' in terms of their health and safety. They must accept that no they cannot run across the road and no they cannot stay out after 9 pm. If you don't stick to 'no' over the little things, how can you expect them to listen to you when you say 'no' to the big things? They will ignore you and do what they want even though this may compromise their safety. As hard as it is 'no' must always mean 'no'.

BE CONSISTENT

Children need stability and structure. They rely upon their parents to keep them safe and to guide them through life. Children get confused when the boundaries move. Every day you hear parents threaten their children with consequences for poor behaviour. How many parents are consistent and follow through with these threats? Parents promise to ground their children, they will take them home from an outing or party, or they will take a toy off them. These threats are to encourage the child to do as they are told and to improve their behaviour. I sat in a restaurant once and heard a father threaten his child nine times to be good and to stop running around and shouting. The child did not listen to her father once. If his threats had been realized she would have had no TV, no bedtime story, no milk, and no play date with her friends. The list went on and on. The child realized that these threats were empty and didn't take them seriously.

If you are going to warn, threaten or bribe your child with something you must follow through. As hard as it may be to take your child's beloved soft toy off them at bedtime you have to accept that it is for the best in the long term. Simply doing this once means that the next time they are naughty and you threaten them with taking their bedtime toy off them they will listen and stop because they know you will stand by your word.

DEVELOP ROUTINE

As parents we hear these words from the moment our child is born. Parents are told to establish a good routine. Most adults get up at the same time every morning. Many will have the same breakfast every morning and go to the same place for lunch every day. Most people love the excitement of the Christmas holidays but also enjoy getting back into their normal routine in the New Year. Children and teenagers are no different. A good routine is essential to giving a child security and stability, and to teaching them about organization, which in turn enables them to become more independent.

Many people face their biggest challenges first thing in the morning, at meal times and at bedtime. A routine will take stress out of these busy times and reduce frustration, boredom and poor behaviour.

Decide what you want your meal time routine to be. If using cutlery and eating a variety of foods is important, then focus on it every time you sit down. If you allow children to eat with their hands or watch TV at the table this will become their routine. Stick with the routine that you want until it becomes the norm. Backing off from it will undo all your hard work, confuse your children and impact on your confidence.

A good routine is essential at night. A child needs sleep to develop and grow and parents need their child to sleep so they can have some 'me' time. To be clear, a routine means doing the same thing at the same time every night. If you want your child to sleep by 7pm then bath them at 6:15pm every night without fail until the routine is established. Only when this happens and the child is sleeping for an adequate amount of time should you relax the routine to accommodate family occasions and outings. Check out Dr Tanya Byron's recommendations for the required sleep a child needs each night. Her book *Little Angels* is a great starting point for establishing a bedtime routine.

 Putting it all together

We live in a culture where the parenting expert and TV personality mould our family life. The 'naughty step' and the 'reward chart' are part of our daily existence. Names such as Gina Ford, Jo Frost, Tracey Hogg and Dr Tanya Byron are often quoted in the playground as the answer to many a parenting problem. Don't be afraid to learn from the parenting experts as they are sharing their experiences, offering support and help and, certainly in the case of Dr Tanya Byron, decades of professional, clinical findings.

It is vital however, that we don't lose touch with who we are and where our strengths lie. If you feel your child needs a more structured routine, use Gina Ford's methods but don't allow them to take over your life. Use the books and the TV programmes as inspiration for new ideas. If you are going to use a particular technique by a parenting expert, use it as it is prescribed. Remember that one size does not fit all. Every child is different. Not every child will respond to the 'naughty step', they may prefer the 'time out' technique.

Be positive, focus on and praise your child's good behaviour and spend less time highlighting their poor behaviour. Give them boundaries and structure if their behaviour does need improving. Remember we make mistakes as parents, but children and teenagers make mistakes too. Ultimately a parent who is confident and positive in themselves is likely to develop a confident and positive child.

50 Sharing your confidence

❝ *Life is a gift, and it offers us the privilege, opportunity, and responsibility to give something back by becoming more.*
Tony Robbins

❝ *Take chances, make mistakes. That's how you grow. Pain nourishes your courage. You have to fail in order to practise being brave.* **Mary Tyler Moore**

❝ *When I do good, I feel good. When I do bad, I feel bad. That's my religion.* **Abraham Lincoln**

❝ *Today is a new beginning, a chance to turn your failures into achievements and your sorrows into so goods. No room for excuses.* **Joel Brown**

❝ *If opportunity doesn't knock, build a door.* **Milton Berle**

This chapter may appear to be a simple reminder to share your learning with others; however it is included firmly as part of your journey to genuine and deep confidence. The benefit to others is a very positive bonus. One of the most powerful and certain ways to anchor learning in your long-term memory is to teach others the things you most want to remember. The fact that you become a force for good as you anchor your learning is a brilliant by-product.

Confidence, like any other state, is contagious. Living it will affect others but sharing your learning and experience will amplify the impact you have on others dramatically. It is useful to remember that reading this book sets you ahead of most other people in your understanding of confidence. Applying the strategies puts you in a very tiny percentage of people who can manage their confidence in any situation. Some might say that it is incumbent on you to share your knowledge with as many people as possible. If this challenges your confidence management then all the more reason to do it!

Use this chapter to prompt questions about the opportunities you can take and make to share your confidence with others. Some of this sharing will be directly from the techniques in the book but I also hope that you have identified some of your own natural confidence strategies. Be sure to share these too; you can now be considered one of the highly confident people referred to throughout the book.

As you have applied these strategies successfully it is possible that you may be seen as little evangelical to others. I don't think that is necessarily a bad thing but find ways to take people with you on the journey. Make the difference for them that you have made for yourself by putting the strategies into action.

TELL YOUR STORY

In Chapter 41 on confident public speaking I encouraged you to find opportunities to speak to varied audiences. Sharing your journey to discover genuine confidence is a great opportunity to embed your confidence and help others to take their own journey.

Tell others why you felt you needed to find or strengthen your confidence. Share what confidence is for you and what it is like when your confidence is strong. Most importantly tell your audience how you made the differences that you did. How did you make the strategies work for you? Advise them of the risks you took and what you might do differently if you had to take the same journey again. Finally share all the reasons why you think they should take their journey to real confidence.

Tell your story at every opportunity and to anyone who is interested. In informal situations use the world's leading expert technique (Chapter 31) and take the opportunity to practise the strategies for remaining calm as you share the details of your journey.

In addition, I would love to hear your journey. If you have applied the techniques in this book and they have made a real difference to you please drop me an email to richard@ twentyoneleadership.com. One of the most rewarding aspects of writing a book like this is hearing the impact that it has made on its readers. I will send a token of my gratitude to everyone who does this.

TEACH THE STRATEGIES

I love people who are confident enough to learn a strategy, put it into practice and then teach that strategy to others. This approach has formed the basis of my way for the last decade. I never teach anything that I haven't practised or tested myself. It's a wonderful way to learn and to help others to learn too.

As you experiment with and apply the strategies contained in this book, make a note of those that you find most powerful and valuable. As they become natural to you review what you did to really bring them to life. Doing this gives you a framework to share them with others and I would be happy if you did so. In the wonderful movie *Pay It Forward* teacher Eugene Simonet (played by Kevin Spacey) sets his class the homework to think of an idea that will change the world then put it into action. Trevor McKinney (Haley Joel Osment) creates the 'Pay It Forward' movement. This means the recipient of a favour does a favour for three others rather than paying the favour back. Each of these three people does three favours and so on and the impact quickly becomes widespread.

Imagine your teaching about confidence having the same impact. If each person who learned a confidence strategy from you, taught it to just three people think of the difference that you would have made to others.

BECOME PART OF A NETWORK

So who do you tell your story to? Who would be interested in learning some confidence strategies? I think with just a little attention and the help of Google you could find a myriad of groups and organizations that you could share your message with. Here are just a few ideas:

- Your local school – either for the pupils or teachers
- Youth clubs – for their leaders
- Beavers, Cubs, Scouts, Rainbows, Brownies, Guides etc.
- Local business speaking groups – YES Groups, Toastmasters
- Regional professional development groups – CIPD, CIM
- Personal development networks

Actively find ways to support others by creating networks of your own. A number of personal fitness trainers in my area hold seminars for their clients where they focus on topics such as confidence. Being part of these networks and sharing your learning is another great way to increase your confidence while helping others to increase theirs.

If you are keen to do this but aren't sure how to start the conversation here are a few simple questions to help you to kick things off.

- Would your members/students/staff find a session on how to be confident in any situation useful?
- If I were able to do this how would you know it has been successful?
- What kinds of things would you like them to say after the event?

These questions will help you to establish the desire from a group and also give an initial indication of the strategies and stories to focus on when you get in front of them.

Highly confident people are generally great networkers. If you haven't been up to this point, make your new-found confidence your reason to build and influence new groups of people.

Putting it all together

One of my favourite paragraphs in any book comes from *Finding Flow* by Mihaly Csikzentmihalyi. It applies perfectly to the difference you can make by sharing your confidence with others.

'Whether we like it or not our lives will leave a mark on the universe. Each person's birth makes ripples that expand in the social environment; parents, siblings, relatives and friends are affected by it, and as we grow up our actions leave a myriad of consequences, some intended, most not. Our consumer decisions make a tiny difference in the economy, political decisions affect the future of the community, and each kind or mean act modifies slightly the total quality of human well-being.'

Your choice isn't whether to make a difference but what difference you make. By taking your learning about confidence from this book and life in general, and sharing it with as wide a group of people as possible in work and your personal life, you are making a significant positive difference.

My experience from studying and working with the highly confident has confirmed beyond doubt that confidence leads not just to success and happiness but to more decisions and actions being taken for the common good. Deep and genuine confidence can change the world. Play your part by accessing your confidence and sharing it with others.

FURTHER READING

Achor, Shawn, *The Happiness Advantage* (Crown Business 2011)

Bersin, Jenny, *Style, the Road to Freedom* (Mike Bersin, 2012)

Buckingham, Marcus, *Now Discover Your Strengths* (Pocket Books 2005)

Byron, Tanya, *Little Angels* (BBC Active 2013)

Cain, Susan, *Quiet: The Power of Introverts in a World That Can't Stop Talking* (Crown 2013)

Covey, Stephen, *The 7 Habits of Highly Effective People* (Free Press 2004)

Csikzentmihalyi, Mihaly, *Finding Flow* by (Basic Books 1998)

Frances-White, Deborah, and Salinsky, Tom, *The Improv Handbook* (Continuum International Publishing Group, 2008)

Genpo, Dennis, *Big Mind Big Heart* (Big Mind Publishing 2007)

Grant, Adam, *Give and Take* (Penguin, 2014)

Hare, Kimberley, *The Trainer's Toolkit: Bringing Brain-friendly Learning to Life* (Crown House Publishing 2005)

Hill, Napoleon, *Think and Grow Rich* (Wilder Publications, 2009)

Imam, Haider, *Straight To Yes* (Capstone 2013)

Jeffers, Susan, *Feel The Fear And Do It Anyway: How to Turn Your Fear and Indecision into Confidence and Action* (Vermilion, 2007).

Kouzes, James, and Posner, Barry, *The Leadership Challenge* (Wiley, 2012)

McKergow, Mark, and Jackson, Paul Z., *The Solutions Focus* (Nicholas Brealey 2006).

Neill, Michael, *You Can Have What You Want* (Hay House UK, 2009)

Pert, Candice, *Molecules of Emotion* (Pocket Books, 1999)

Wiseman, Richard, *The Luck Factor* (Randomhouse, 2004).

WEBLINKS

Chapter 30

Money saving expert website: http://www.moneysavingexpert.com/family/stop-spending-budgeting-tool

Chapter 23

Learn more about Dr Cuddy here: http://www.hbs.edu/faculty/Pages/profile.aspx?facId=491042

Listen to Dr Cuddy's TED Talk at: http://www.ted.com/talks/amy_cuddy_your_body_language_shapes_who_you_are.html

Chapter 45

Listen to the brilliant Sir Ken Robinson's 2006 TED Talk 'How schools kill creativity' at: http://www.ted.com/talks/ken_robinson_says_schools_kill_creativity.html

Read Dr Gardner's paper 'In a nutshell' at: http://howardgardner01.files.wordpress.com/2012/06/in-a-nutshell-minh.pdf

NOTES

Discover the secrets behind greatness